tch the games, fill in the scores, and follow the unfold
.he FIFA Women's World Cup Canada 2015.

~OUP E

		SCORE		
JUNE 9, 4:00 PM	SPAIN			MONTREAL COSTA RICA
JUNE 9, 7:00 PM	BRAZIL			MONTREAL KOREA REPUBLIC
JUNE 13, 4:00 PM	BRAZIL			MONTREAL SPAIN
JUNE 13, 7:00 PM	~REA REPUBLIC			MONTREAL COSTA RICA
JUNE 17, 7:00 PM	~REA REPUBLIC			OTTAWA SPAIN
JUNE 17, 8:00 PM	COSTA RICA			MONCTON BRAZIL

~M	P	W	D	L	F	A	PTS

GROUP F

		SCORE		
JUNE 9, 2:00 PM	FRANCE			MONCTON ENGLAND
JUNE 9, 5:00 PM	COLOMBIA			MONCTON MEXICO
JUNE 13, 2:00 PM	FRANCE			MONCTON COLOMBIA
JUNE 13, 5:00 PM	ENGLAND			MONCTON MEXICO
JUNE 17, 4:00 PM	MEXICO			OTTAWA FRANCE
JUNE 17, 4:00 PM	ENGLAND			MONTREAL COLOMBIA

TEAM	P	W	D	L	F	A	PTS

KEY NOTES FOR THE MATCH SCHEDULE

Notes for deciding the group stages

P = played (each team plays three group matches); W = won; D = draw; L = lost; F = goals scored (for); A = goals conceded (against); Pts = points. Three points for a win; one for a draw; no points for a loss.

After most points, groups are decided first by better positive goal difference, then the total goals scored. After this, the head-to-head results will decide the order. If three teams are involved, again the goal difference in these matches decides, then the total goals scored. If teams are still equal, then the FIFA Organising Committee will use a lottery to draw teams.

Explanation of knockout stages

All knockout matches will be decided on the day they are played. If the scores are even after 90 minutes, extra time (two 15-minute periods) will be allotted for play. If the scores again remain even, penalty kicks (a penalty shoot-out) will decide the winner. Teams will take five shots each, alternately, unless one team cannot win after three or four attempts. If the scores are still even after 10 attempts, then a sudden-death shoot-out follows, decided by the first team to score.

©FIFA

FIFA
WOMEN'S
WORLD CUP
CANADA
2015 ™

THE OFFICIAL BOOK

Text by Catherine Etoe, Jen O'Neill, and
Natalia Sollohub

For the original edition:
Project director: Martin Corteel
Project art editor: Luke Griffin
Picture research: Paul Langan
Book designer: Harj Ghundale
Production: Maria Petalidou

For the American edition:
Editor: Nicole Lanctot
Production manager: Louise Kurtz
Layout: Ada Rodriguez
Proofreader: Miranda Ottewell

First published in the United States of
America in 2015 by Abbeville Press,
137 Varick Street, New York, NY 10013

First published in Great Britain in 2015 by
Carlton Books Limited, 20 Mortimer Street,
London W1T 3JW

First edition
10 9 8 7 6 5 4 3 2 1

ISBN 978-0-7892-1228-3

Library of Congress Cataloging-in-
Publication Data available upon request

For bulk or premium sales and for text
adoption procedures, write to Customer
Service Manager, Abbeville Press,
137 Varick Street, New York, NY 10013,
or call 1-800-Artbook.

Visit Abbeville Press online at
www.abbeville.com.

FIFA
WOMEN'S
WORLD CUP
CANADA
2015
™

THE OFFICIAL BOOK

CONTENTS

ghing in at nearly four pounds, the FIFA Women's World Cup
hy is light enough to be lifted by an individual, but it takes
uad of 23 players to win it.

WELCOME TO CANADA

Canada loves its soccer, and its women's side has been its most successful team in recent times. Now this stunning country has the opportunity to showcase its passion for the beautiful game to the rest of the soccer-playing world. From coast to coast, featuring six culturally diverse cities and their superb sporting venues, Canada will welcome the 23 other competing nations, their fans, and the media when it hosts 2015's biggest festival of soccer—the FIFA Women's World Cup.

An aerial view of downtown Vancouver and BC Place, the venue for the final, nestled within Vancouver Harbour.

TO A GREATER GOAL™

For sports, for women, and for the host nation, this tournament features the best of the best and the opportunity to carry that positive message and journey forward.

Canada is not only a vast country with astonishing vistas, it is also a proud sporting nation—and soccer is the country's biggest participation sport. The Canadian Soccer Association celebrated its centenary in 2012, the same year that its women's team won bronze at the London Olympics, reinforcing the Canucks's standing as one of the world's top-ranked teams.

Now it is Canada's turn to welcome the best teams in the world as it hosts the premier FIFA women's soccer tournament; 128 nations are entered, all with ambitions of competing in the finals, but only 24 teams have a chance to fulfill the ultimate dream of victory in Vancouver on July 5.

With home advantage, the hopeful hosts believe that they are genuine contenders to win the cup for the first time. But Canada won't be the only ones confident of creating waves—many teams have their hungry eyes on the prize, including neighbors USA and European powerhouse

Germany, both two-time winners, as well as current holders Japan and the likes of Sweden and France.

Canada has gotten close before, of course—it was a semifinalist in the USA in 2003. The team has produced some heroines in the women's game, too, such as super-striker Charmaine Hooper, warrior-like Andrea Neil, and charismatic midfielder Kara Lang, one of the Canada 2015 Official Ambassadors, her career sadly cut short by injury.

Canada's influence in the women's game is not limited to its players, either; it has produced pioneering officials like FIFA's former Head of Women's Referee Development, Sonia Denoncourt, and Carol Anne Chenard, the first woman to referee at England's Wembley Stadium.

Having attended the inaugural FIFA U-19 Women's World Championship in 2002, then the FIFA U-20 World Cup 2007 in record numbers, and cheered on its young

representatives at the slickly organized FIFA U-20 Women's World Cup 2014, the nation's citizens are once again being urged to support their team and welcome visitors as they enjoy Canada's natural wonders, culture, and hospitality.

Providing a stage for these world-class athletes gives Canadians the opportunity to celebrate not only the prestigious competition itself but also all female players across the globe. The tournament official slogan, "To a Greater Goal," encapsulates this vision of recognizing and lauding the current generation of soccer greats, along with inspiring and empowering the next.

"For sport, for women, for Canada: those are three qualities that highlight our ambitions in hosting a successful FIFA Women's World Cup," says Victor Montagliani, chairman of the National Organizing Committee and president of Canadian Soccer Association.

For Canada, and for the wider game, over success would mean an explosion in interest similar to the legacy of the FIFA Women's World Cup in the USA in 1999, matched with the superb quality of play, on-field drama, joyously intense atmospheres experienced Germany in 2011.

If the Land of the Maple Leaf steps up to the plate as expected, then whichever team lifts the trophy on July 5, Canada, soccer will all be winners.

Left: **Canada coach John Herdman holds up the tournament's official slogan, and many ways its mission statement: To a Greater Goal.**

Right: **The official mascot of the tournament Shueme the Great White Owl.**

THE QUALIFYING TRAIL

Before a ball has even been kicked, it is safe to say that this FIFA Women's World Cup will be an exceptional one. For this edition, the tournament will throw together 24 competing nations for the first time in its history.

Eight of those are debut teams, others have been ever-present, and still more hope that this can be their breakthrough moment on the world stage—as will every player who gets the chance to represent them on the pitches of Canada this summer. All will have worked their socks off to be a part of it—and all know that, whatever happens in the weeks that follow, they have reached the pinnacle of the women's game.

To hit those heights, most have experienced the agonies and ecstasies of qualification—hard-fought campaigns that raged over six continents and featured 128 teams in a total of 398 matches. The first of those kicked off in April 2013 and the very last was played in December 2014, with Ecuador bagging the final spot on offer a mere four days before the eagerly awaited tournament draw in Ottawa.

Fittingly, Japan was one of the first to book its tickets to Canada alongside

Australia, China PR, Korea Republic, and newcomer Thailand, who was in dreamland after holding its nerve against Vietnam on its opponents' home soil to claim the fifth Asian Football Confederation spot.

Seven of Europe's eight entrants were next to reach Canada, but it was not a quick journey; the yearlong qualification groups kicked off in September 2013. The majority made light work of their rivals, though, with finals newcomer Switzerland becoming the first to qualify, in June 2014, with two games to spare. England, France, Germany, and Norway went through with a game to go, as did Spain, who will now make its finals bow.

Perennial finalist Sweden was made to fight for its place by Scotland, but that rivalry was settled in September 2014 when a lively crowd and its "Camp Sweden" fans cheered the Blågult to victory over the Scots in Gothenburg. It took playoffs

to decide the final coveted European pla[ce] four of the best runners-up battling it ou[t] home and away, with the Netherlands going on to put its name in the draw for the first time ever in November 2014.

The months before had seen a frenzy o[f] action among the four other confederati[ons] as each hosted its qualifying tournamen[t.] It was a straightforward job for respectiv[e] champions USA, Brazil, New Zealand, an[d] Nigeria, all so regularly dominant forces [in] their continents; joining them in reachin[g] Canada 2015 were Mexico and Colombi[a] and maiden finals nations Cameroon, Cô[te] d'Ivoire, and Costa Rica.

The final piece of the jigsaw is Canad[a, of] course. As hosts, the Canucks automatic[ally] qualified for the tournament they had graced five times previously. The nation expects its team to go all the way this ti[me,] but supporters of the 23 others have hig[h] hopes, too. Only one nation can win, but[,] after the manifold efforts that have gon[e] into getting this far, all will do their utm[ost] to make their country proud.

Left: **Switzerland's Ana Maria Crnogorcevi[c] (13) jumps for the ball with Denmark goalkeeper Stina Lykke Petersen during the FIFA Women's World Cup Canada 201[5] Group C qualification match in Aarau. The game ended 1–1, the only goal Switzerlan[d] conceded and the only point it dropped.**

Right: **The United States's Carli Lloyd is congratulated by Megan Rapinoe. Lloyd scored five goals and won the Golden Ba[ll] for best player at the 2014 CONCACAF Women's Championship.**

THE VENUES

From coast to coast, in six vibrant host cities surrounded by stunning scenery, Canada provides the perfect setting for the FIFA Women's World Cup 2015.

Extending from the Atlantic to the Pacific and northward to the Arctic, Canada's enormous landmass (the second-largest country in the world, behind Russia) encompasses 10 provinces, three territories, and six time zones. Its population of 35 million is officially bilingual, ethnically diverse, and warmly welcoming. And its awe-inspiring natural geography makes it the perfect destination for landscape lovers and alfresco adventurers.

Matches at the FIFA Women's World Cup 2015 will be played in six dynamic cities stretching from coast to coast. Some of the venues for 2015 are home to both soccer and gridiron football teams, and all 52 games will be played on artificial turf rather than grass, fields that meet the FIFA 2-Star soccer turf requirements (ensuring the highest-playing performance for professional-level soccer) to guarantee an equitable standard of surface for all teams. And goal-line technology will be in place for the first time ever in a women's competition.

The standard of host stadiums is high, too, with the climax set to be played in the nation's premier soccer venue, the beautiful BC Place, home to the Whitecaps FC soccer team in Vancouver, British Columbia. Reopened in 2011 after a $563 million makeover, including the installation of the largest cable-supported retractable roof of its kind anywhere, BC Place lies in the midst of Vancouver's entertainment district and is set to host nine matches, including the final.

Eleven games, including the tournament opener, will kick off in front of the green and gold seats of the Edmonton Eskimos in the Commonwealth Stadium, Edmonton, Alberta—a fitting opening venue given the phenomenal support for soccer in the city. The folks of Edmonton turned out in record numbers—47,784—to witness Canada taking on USA in the final of the first-ever FIFA U-19 Women's World Championship in 2002, still the biggest crowd at a FIFA youth women's match.

Heading eastward to the "cultural cradle of Canada," we reach another host venue, Winnipeg Stadium, which opened in 2013. Winnipeg, Manitoba, hosted Canada's first-ever women's national team camp, on Canada Day, July 1, 1986, and the first women's home international friendly on July 23, 1990.

Ottawa, Ontario, is the country's capital and a hotbed for the game, offering leagues for players of all ages and skill levels. Ottawa's stadium was renovated in July 2014, and while it is one of the smaller venues, its fans will no doubt create a fantastic atmosphere.

Moving on to Montreal, Quebec, we reach the imposing Olympic Stadium otherwise known as "The Big O." Host to Major League Soccer team Montreal Impact, this iconic landmark will be a lively location for nine games, including a semifinal.

Last and farthest east, but certainly not least, is Moncton, New Brunswick, Canada' first officially bilingual city and host to seven matches. Moncton Stadium, set on the campus of the Université de Moncton, is a compact arena, but it is also ideal for creating a buzz and sense of occasion.

This is North America's third FIFA Women's World Cup but Canada's first, and the nation is more than ready.

Below: **Canada will play China PR in the tournament opener in the Commonwealth Stadium, Edmonton.**

VANCOUVER

ritish Columbia

C Place Stadium

apacity: **54,500**

WINNIPEG

Manitoba

Winnipeg Stadium

Capacity: **40,000**

MONTREAL

Quebec

Olympic Stadium

Capacity: **66,308**

MONCTON

New Brunswick

Moncton Stadium

Capacity: **20,725**

EDMONTON

berta

ommonwealth Stadium

apacity: **56,302**

OTTAWA

Ontario

Lansdowne Stadium

Capacity: **40,000**

CANADA
2015

FIFA
WOMEN'S WORLD CUP
TM©

FIFA WOMEN'S WORLD CUP
CANADA 2015™

FIFA
WOMEN'S
WORLD CUP
TM©

THE DRAW

Officials, coaches, and media came together in the culturally rich surroundings of the Canadian Museum of History in Ottawa in December 2014 to witness a crucial part of the FIFA Women's World Cup 2015—the draw.

Performing the task in front of a worldwide television audience and a packed auditorium were Jerome Valcke, FIFA Secretary General, and Tatjana Haenni, FIFA Head of Women's Football, assisted by a selection of inspirational Canadian sporting stars.

There were gasps almost immediately as it transpired that host Canada, its distinctive red ball deliberately plucked out first, would face coach John Herdman's former charge New Zealand.

"They represent a lot to me," was his beaming response. "So to have the opportunity to share a moment with them in Canada is really great."

China PR was also in the mix in Group A and it will share Canada's own great moment when the two kick off the tournament in Edmonton.

Current holder Japan bagged a group with three first-timers, while England was picked alongside its 2011 adversaries, France. Meanwhile 2007 winner Germany was matched up with its UEFA Women's Euro 2013 final opponents, Norway.

The biggest drama, though, came when USA, Sweden, former Asian champion Australia, and African giants Nigeria were picked together to earn Group D the inevitable "group of death" moniker.

Sweden coach Pia Sundhage, who led USA to silver in 2011, was optimistic. "It good to play against the best teams in t group stage, though," she said. "We're looking at it positively."

Below: **Tatjana Haenni and Jerome Valcke, the center, oversee the completed draw the FIFA Women's World Cup Canada 201 front of a rapt audience.**

Right: **An officer of the Royal Canadian Mounted Police carries the nearly 18-inch FIFA Women's World Cup trophy at the dra**

MATCH SCHEDULE

Watch the games, fill in the scores, and follow the unfolding drama and excitement of the FIFA Women's World Cup Canada 2015.

GROUP A

		SCORE		
JUNE 6, 4:00 PM			EDMONTON	
CANADA			**CHINA PR**	
JUNE 6, 7:00 PM			EDMONTON	
NEW ZEALAND			**NETHERLANDS**	
JUNE 11, 4:00 PM			EDMONTON	
CHINA PR			**NETHERLANDS**	
JUNE 11, 7:00 PM			EDMONTON	
CANADA			**NEW ZEALAND**	
JUNE 15, 6:30 PM			WINNIPEG	
CHINA PR			**NEW ZEALAND**	
JUNE 15, 7:30 PM			MONTREAL	
NETHERLANDS			**CANADA**	

TEAM	P	W	D	L	GD	PTS

GROUP B

		SCORE		
JUNE 7, 1:00 PM			OTTAWA	
NORWAY			**THAILAND**	
JUNE 7, 4:00 PM			OTTAWA	
GERMANY			**CÔTE D'IVOIRE**	
JUNE 11, 4:00 PM			OTTAWA	
GERMANY			**NORWAY**	
JUNE 11, 7:00 PM			OTTAWA	
CÔTE D'IVOIRE			**THAILAND**	
JUNE 15, 3:00 PM			WINNIPEG	
THAILAND			**GERMANY**	
JUNE 15, 5:00 PM			MONCTON	
CÔTE D'IVOIRE			**NORWAY**	

TEAM	P	W	D	L	GD	PT

GROUP C

		SCORE		
JUNE 8, 4:00 PM			VANCOUVER	
CAMEROON			**ECUADOR**	
JUNE 8, 7:00 PM			VANCOUVER	
JAPAN			**SWITZERLAND**	
JUNE 12, 4:00 PM			VANCOUVER	
SWITZERLAND			**ECUADOR**	
JUNE 12, 7:00 PM			VANCOUVER	
JAPAN			**CAMEROON**	
JUNE 16, 3:00 PM			EDMONTON	
SWITZERLAND			**CAMEROON**	
JUNE 16, 4:00 PM			WINNIPEG	
ECUADOR			**JAPAN**	

TEAM	P	W	D	L	GD	PTS

GROUP D

		SCORE		
JUNE 8, 3:00 PM			WINNIPEG	
SWEDEN			**NIGERIA**	
JUNE 8, 6:30 PM			WINNIPEG	
USA			**AUSTRALIA**	
JUNE 12, 4:00 PM			WINNIPEG	
AUSTRALIA			**NIGERIA**	
JUNE 12, 7:00 PM			WINNIPEG	
USA			**SWEDEN**	
JUNE 16, 5:00 PM			VANCOUVER	
NIGERIA			**USA**	
JUNE 16, 6:00 PM			EDMONTON	
AUSTRALIA			**SWEDEN**	

TEAM	P	W	D	L	GD	PT

GROUP E

	SCORE	
JUNE 9, 4:00 PM		MONTREAL
SPAIN		**COSTA RICA**
JUNE 9, 7:00 PM		MONTREAL
BRAZIL		**KOREA REPUBLIC**
JUNE 13, 4:00 PM		MONTREAL
BRAZIL		**SPAIN**
JUNE 13, 7:00 PM		MONTREAL
KOREA REPUBLIC		**COSTA RICA**
JUNE 17, 7:00 PM		OTTAWA
KOREA REPUBLIC		**SPAIN**
JUNE 17, 8:00 PM		MONCTON
COSTA RICA		**BRAZIL**

TEAM	P	W	D	L	GD	PTS

GROUP F

	SCORE	
JUNE 9, 2:00 PM		MONCTON
FRANCE		**ENGLAND**
JUNE 9, 5:00 PM		MONCTON
COLOMBIA		**MEXICO**
JUNE 13, 2:00 PM		MONCTON
FRANCE		**COLOMBIA**
JUNE 13, 5:00 PM		MONCTON
ENGLAND		**MEXICO**
JUNE 17, 4:00 PM		OTTAWA
MEXICO		**FRANCE**
JUNE 17, 4:00 PM		MONTREAL
ENGLAND		**COLOMBIA**

TEAM	P	W	D	L	GD	PTS

ROUND OF 16

(39)	JUNE 20, 4:00 PM	SCORE	OTTAWA
1B			**3ACD**
(37)	JUNE 20, 5:30 PM		EDMONTON
2A			**2C**
(41)	JUNE 21, 2:00 PM		MONCTON
1E			**2D**
(40)	JUNE 21, 4:00 PM		MONTREAL
1F			**2E**

(44)	JUNE 21, 4:30 PM	SCORE	VANCOUVER
1A			**3CDE**
(43)	JUNE 22, 5:00 PM		OTTAWA
2B			**2F**
(38)	JUNE 22, 6:00 PM		EDMONTON
1D			**3BEF**
(42)	JUNE 23, 7:00 PM		VANCOUVER
1C			**3ABF**

QUARTERFINALS

(46)	JUNE 26, 4:00 PM	SCORE	MONTREAL
W39			**W40**
(45)	JUNE 26, 7:30 PM		OTTAWA
W37			**W38**

(47)	JUNE 27, 4:00 PM	SCORE	EDMONTON
W41			**W42**
(48)	JUNE 27, 4:30 PM		VANCOUVER
W43			**W44**

SEMIFINALS

(49)	JUNE 30, 7:00 PM	SCORE	MONTREAL
W45			**W46**
(50)	JULY 1, 5:00 PM		EDMONTON
W47			**W48**

THIRD PLACE

	JULY 4, 2:00 PM	SCORE	EDMONTON
L49			**L50**

FINAL

	JULY 5, 4:00 PM	SCORE	VANCOUVER
W49			**W50**

times are local

MEET THE TEAMS

To perform and excel on the world stage is surely the dream of any player, and success at the FIFA Women's World Cup represents the apex of a female soccer player's career. For some teams making their first appearances at the tournament, qualification was an achievement in itself; for others nothing but outright victory will suffice. From established masters of the elite game to ambitious new stars ready to shine, here are the 24 teams that make up Canada 2015.

Japan's ecstatic players revel in the moment of being crowned the best in the world in Frankfurt, July 2011. Four years on, with 23 other teams vying for that title, can they repeat that success?

The seating at Edmonton's Commonwealth
Stadium boasts the colors of the Edmonton
Eskimos, the Canadian Football League tea

CANADA
2015
FIFA
WOMEN'S WORLD CUP
TM©

GROUP A

ll eyes will be on Canada's opener in Edmonton
gainst China PR, with the Canucks as the victors
 the two teams' only previous FIFA Women's
World Cup meeting, in 2003. China has beaten
ew Zealand twice before, while the Netherlands
mains an unknown quantity and could be the dark
orse of the group.

CANADA

CAN THE HOST GO ALL THE WAY?

As host of the FIFA Women's World Cup 2015, Canada was spared the pressures of th CONCACAF qualifying tournament. The Canucks, though, will still be expected to hit the ground running when the tournament kicks off on home soil in June.

COACH

JOHN HERDMAN

From County Durham, this charismatic Englishman has experience in senior tournament soccer, having coached New Zealand in two editions of the FIFA Women's World Cup and at the 2008 Olympics in Beijing. He is noted for instilling a professional mentality and strong learning environment into the Football Ferns. He took over Canada after the departure of Carolina Morace in 2011 and was nominated for FIFA coach of the year in 2012. Touted as a possible replacement for England manager Hope Powell in 2013, he has since signed a long-term contract with Canada until 2020. He is prepared to give youth a chance and has declared that host Canada has to go all out to lift the World Cup in 2015.

Having finished an impressive fourth in the FIFA Women's World Cup 2003 and with a rising reputation, Canada surprisingly stuttered in the following editions, despite the promise offered by its clinching of the CONCACAF title in 2010.

However, under Englishman John Herdman, who took over at the helm soon after the FIFA Women's World Cup 2011, the team quickly returned to winning ways.

A historic gold medal performance at the Pan American Games in Mexico in 2011 gave Canada the chance to catch its breath after it was knocked out of contention in its pointless FIFA Women's World Cup that year. And its subsequent display in the London 2012 Olympic Games showed the world that the elite teams still have the

capacity to breathe new life into the sp Canada's performance in an exhilaratin end-to-end Olympic semifinal defeat by neighbors and rivals the USA at Old Trafford will live long in the memory of soccer fans of all nations.

And as the Canucks filed onto the pitch at Wembley Stadium to collect their med after beating France to bronze, there was genuine appreciation for their efforts tha summer. They will look to up their medal count this summer and have prepared wi friendlies against the top teams in the w including Germany, the USA, and Japan.

The Canucks team will experience the m intensity of pressure and support that be the host side brings.

KEY PLAYER

CHRISTINE SINCLAIR
Born: June 12, 1983

Earning her first senior appearance at the age of 16, Sinclair has gone on to win more than 200 caps for her country. Big, strong, and determined, she is a clinical finisher from any part of the park. In 2010 she became only the tenth female player to score 100 international goals. Described by her coach John Herdman as a "Rolls-Royce" of a player, the Canucks' captain leads by example. Top scorer and a flag bearer for Canada at the close of the London 2012 Olympics, she remains humble despite her legendary status in the women's game. She's has won 12 Canadian soccer Player of the Year titles plus nominations for FIFA Women's World Player of the Year. In 2013 she signed for Portland Thorns (returning to the city where she had a stellar college career) in the US National Women's Soccer League.

WORLD CUP RECORD

Year	Venue	Result
1991	China	Did not qualify
1995	Sweden	Group stage (3rd, Group B)
1999	USA	Group stage (3rd, Group C)
2003	USA	Fourth Place
2007	China	Group stage (3rd, Group C)
2011	Germany	Group stage (4th, Group A)

e squad's youngsters were kept on ir toes when they featured in the FIFA 0 Women's World Cup 2014 in Canada. andful of the players who made it to quarterfinals of that competition— impressive center-back Kadeisha hanan—have a strong chance for success in the senior tournament. Their experience of playing in front of expectant home crowds will be invaluable.

And while Herdman has been keen to introduce teenagers in his senior setup— four players were 18 years old and under in the 2–1 friendly loss to Germany in June 2014—the core of his team played in the FIFA Women's World Cup 2011.

Those veterans will offer stability to the squad, but Herdman has called for the twelfth player to step up in 2015. "Don't just come and watch us," he told Canadians. "Come out and support us and help us win the FIFA Women's World Cup."

LOOK OUT FOR

RIN MCLEOD
Born: February 26, 1983
Position: Goalkeeper

McCleod is a super shot-stopper who as been playing soccer since the age of our. Acrobatic, quick, and commanding, he is a safe pair of hands and has the onfidence and trust of her defensive ne. In 2012 she won Olympic bronze nd her positional play, reliability, and decision-making were praised in the ubsequent technical report. Named in he All-Time Canada XI women's team n 2012, she was the Canucks' player of he match in the 2–1 friendly loss to Germany in June 2014.

JESSIE FLEMING
Born: March 11, 1998
Position: Midfielder

Fifteen years old when she made her senior debut in December 2013, Fleming has represented Canada in the 2014 FIFA U-17 and U-20 Women's World Cups. A fine athlete who started playing soccer at age three, she loves to get on the ball, reads the game superbly, and can pick a pass and link play. She tasted tournament action on home soil with the U-20s in 2014, and will not be overawed if Herdman gives her the chance in the senior competition this summer.

DESIREE SCOTT
Born: July 31, 1987
Position: Midfielder

An experienced player who relishes her nickname "Destroyer," and is another product of Canada's youth system, Scott debuted for the seniors at age 22 in February 2010 and was part of the Cyprus Cup winning team that year. Featured in the FIFA Women's World Cup 2011, she has flourished under Herdman. She was a key member of the Pan American Games gold medal team that year and shone at London 2012. In 2014, she joined Notts County in the English FA Women's Super League.

CHINA PR
YOUNG STEEL ROSES LOOKING TO BLOSSOM THIS SUMMER

Some nations are perennial performers at the FIFA Women's World Cup, and China PR was one of those until it missed out in 2011. Now they are back—but how will the Steel Roses fare in Canada?

COACH

HAO WEI

Wei was appointed head coach after China missed out on qualification to both the FIFA Women's World Cup 2011 and London 2012 Olympics—so the heat was on in the AFC Women's Asian Cup. The former defender rode the challenge, staying calm as China finished third and qualified for 2015. Still only 38, he boasts a wealth of playing experience in the Chinese league and has coached men but seems to be relishing his involvement in the women's game. In July 2014 he traveled to the northeast of England to meet English FA Women's Super League side Sunderland Ladies and share ideas on soccer development.

China's record in the top women's tournament is a decent one; it has never come away from the biggest stage of all without reaching at least the quarterfinals, and in 1999 it almost took the title—only to lose on penalties to the USA.

Its form has fluctuated since those heady days, and it was absent completely when Japan narrowly beat it to a qualification in the FIFA Women's World Cup 2011, but it has consciously rebuilt with youth, and so it goes into 2015 with the hopes of a nation behind it after gaining qualification with its best finish in the AFC Women's Asian Cup since 2008.

In May 2014 the tournament in Vietnam was the key to qualification in Asia, and China automatically booked its place in Canada when it finished runner-up in it group.

Beating relative minnows Thailand an Myanmar and then drawing with a tou Korea Republic meant it was job done, but China, with its proud tradition in th women's game, wanted to achieve mor Coach Hao Wei's team also wanted to g winning momentum under way in the le up to Canada 2015.

The Steel Roses did their utmost to remain unbeaten but lost 2–1 to old riv Japan in the semifinals, in a tense matc that was agonizingly settled by a goal i

The new look China PR team has the hon of opening the tournament against Cana in Edmonton.

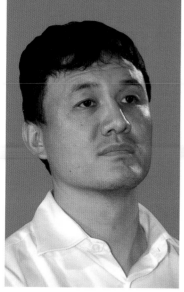

KEY PLAYER

YANG LI
Born: January 31, 1991

They call her the new Sun Wen, and she is most definitely a goal-getter in the mold of China's all-time highest-scoring legend. Strong in the air, she has a lethal technique, but is no showboater and can grab scrappy goals from close range or pounce to punish sloppy passing. She first came to prominence at the invitational Four Nations Tournament, which China won in 2014. She established herself in the senior side during the Algarve Cup and showed her goal-scoring prowess when it mattered in the qualifying competition for Canada 2015, the AFC Women's Asian Cup. The Jiangsu Huatai player finished the tournament as joint top scorer with six goals, including the winner against Korea Republic that saw China take third place overall.

WORLD CUP RECORD

Year	Venue	Result
1991	China	Quarterfinalists
1995	Sweden	Fourth place
1999	USA	Runner-up
2003	USA	Quarterfinalists
2007	China	Quarterfinalists
2011	Germany	Did not qualify

dying moments of extra time. e players still left a hot and humid Ho Minh City with their heads held high, ugh, after beating a talented Korea ublic by a late-late goal in the match hird place three days later.
  io has shown faith in youngsters, ling a side whose average age was 23

in the competition, and believes that China has a team for the future on its hands.
  "It gives me hope that there's a great foundation to improve upon in the future," says Hao, adding that work to plot China's buildup to Canada was under way.
  Three years of working on the players' game as a group has led to them gaining

a sound grasp of their individual and collective defensive duties. When deployed, it is a system that can contain threatening opponents, while it has the additional armory to hit teams swiftly and with potency, on the break.
  That China narrowly failed to go beyond the quarterfinals of the Asian Games in September 2014 is perhaps a sign that it is still a work in progress. Canada 2015 will certainly be another yardstick for this developing team.

LOOK OUT FOR

HANG YUE
Born: September 30, 1990
Position: Goalkeeper

dependable and intelligent keeper hose height and clever positioning ake her a tough opponent to beat, hang showed her potential at the FIFA -20 Women's World Cup 2008 and has one on to become first-choice number 1, aining further high-intensity experience t annual friendly tournaments such as e Four Nations invitational and Algarve up. She kept three clean sheets in group lay at the AFC Women's Asian Cup in May 2014, ultimately conceding just three oals in five matches.

WU HAIYAN
Born: February 26, 1993
Position: Defender

An influential captain, Wu commands the defense from the center, but can do a job at right-back, too. Calm and collected, she plays with a maturity beyond her years and is a reliable leader. She made her senior debut in 2011 and gained valuable tournament experience at the FIFA U-20 Women's World Cup 2012. She was a key player in China's Algarve Cup campaign in 2014 and ever-present in the AFC Women's Asian Cup matches that secured China's qualification for Canada 2015.

MA XIAOXU
Born: June 5, 1988
Position: Forward

Dubbed a teenage sensation before China's last FIFA Women's World Cup outing when it hosted the tournament, "Lady Wayne Rooney" will celebrate her 27th birthday in Canada. She scored the goals that saw China win the AFC Women's Asian Cup in 2006 and won the Golden Ball and Shoe at the FIFA U-20 Women's World Championship the same year. She has also played in Sweden's highly respected Damallsvenskan. With such a background, she could now be ready to fulfill her considerable promise.

NEW ZEALAND
FOOTBALL FERNS READY TO REALIZE POTENTIAL

New Zealand has made impressive strides since the FIFA Women's World Cup in 2011. As they head to their third consecutive finals, the Football Ferns will be ambitious to do more than make up the numbers.

COACH

TONY READINGS

Readings played at a non-league level for AFC Wimbledon in his homeland of England before moving to play with North Shore United in New Zealand. He was assistant to current Canada coach John Herdman at the FIFA Women's World Cup in 2011, as well as the 2008 Olympics. The 39-year-old has a great understanding of the potential of his young squad, having managed the Junior Football Ferns at the FIFA U-20 Women's World Cup in 2010. He took full control of the senior side in the lead-up to the London 2012 Olympic Games, where they registered their first international finals tournament win with a 3–1 victory over Cameroon.

Rather, New Zealand will hope to better their current record of having collected one point in the competition—against Mexico in 2011—by building upon more recent outings against the best nations in the world.

Notable results have included a quarter-final qualification in the London 2012 Olympics, where the team lost 2–0 to eventual winners USA, and victories over Brazil and China PR to lift the inaugural Valais Women's Cup in Switzerland in September 2013.

The Ferns also went on to narrowly lose 2–1 to world champions Japan in a friendly in May 2014, before drawing in a double-header with Brazil the following month.

They staked their place in the FIFA Women's World Cup in October 2014 with a convincing show in their qualification tournament, the OFC Women's Nations C The Kiwis scored 30 goals without reply three games, although plucky host Papua New Guinea kept the score down to 3–0 its encounter with Tony Readings's team, who won the tournament to make it a record fifth OFC Women's Nations Cup ti

Skipper Abby Erceg said afterward that the competition had been a good test for the Ferns and an indicator of the areas th needed to be worked on ahead of their arrival in Canada.

The Football Ferns of New Zealand are super fit and always give their all, to the very end.

ROSIE WHITE
Born: June 6, 1993

A strong, direct striker, White likes to wear the number 13 shirt and was regarded as a soccer prodigy when she hit a hat trick against Colombia in the FIFA U-17 Women's World Cup 2008. She scored three more for the Junior Football Ferns against host Chile at the FIFA U-20 edition just 18 days later. Fast-tracked into the seniors, the multiple New Zealand Football Young Player of the Year winner made her debut as a 15-year-old against China in 2009. Her performances at the FIFA U-20 Women's World Cup 2010 earned her a scholarship at the University of California, Los Angeles, where she has learned, grown—and scored goals. Awarded the Golden Ball for best player in the OFC Women's Nations Cup, she has a raft of tournament experience.

WORLD CUP RECORD

Year	Venue	Result
1991	China	Group stage (4th, Group A)
1995	Sweden	Did not qualify
1999	USA	Did not qualify
2003	USA	Did not qualify
2007	China	Group stage (4th, Group D)
2011	Germany	Group stage (4th, Group B)

think the most exciting thing heading
is World Cup is the real prospect of us
g a true threat to the top nations and
ng how far we can push ourselves and
performance," she added.
the top nation in Oceania, New Zealand
finitely a dominant force within its own

confederation, and its gutsy approach and competitive nature typifies its attitude to the game. But that style is still developing as players come together for more frequent international camps, friendlies, and tournaments, and an increasing number garner experience of league soccer in Europe and Asia.

As Canada 2015 draws near, other nations in the world are starting to notice that the Kiwis' athletic, never-say-die attitude is now complemented by greater finesse and tactical awareness.

With a string of testing friendlies taking the Ferns all the way through to the summer, Oceania's number-one team should be ready to set new records for all the world to see.

OOK OUT FOR

LI RILEY
orn: October 30, 1987
osition: Defender

n athletic wingback, Riley was born
California but is eligible to represent
ew Zealand because her father is a
wi. She has spent the majority of her
reer in the United States, most
otably with FC Gold Pride in the
Women's Professional Soccer league
nd then with Western New York Flash
their WPS Championship–winning
eason of 2011. Veteran of two FIFA
omen's World Cups and two
lympics, she joined LdB FC Malmo
ow FC Rosengard) in Sweden in
012, winning titles with both.

ABBY ERCEG
Born: November 20, 1989
Position: Defender

Captain since 2013, Erceg debuted in 2006 and has since been a virtual fixture, becoming the first player, male or female, to win 100 caps for New Zealand. Following her New Zealand Football Young Player of the Year award in 2007, she received the NZF Players' Player accolade in 2011. A true leader on and off the field, she is another Fern who enjoys her club soccer overseas, having competed in both the Frauen-Bundesliga in Germany and the USA's National Women's Soccer League.

AMBER HEARN
Born: November 28, 1984
Position: Forward

This powerful "fox in the box" has played in England (Doncaster Belles and Arsenal), Canada (Ottawa Fury), and Germany (FF USV Jena). She made her senior international debut in February 2004 and went on to be named NZF Women's Player of the Year. She has appeared in two Olympics and one FIFA Women's World Cup for the Football Ferns, netting against Japan in both tournaments. She scored the most goals at the 2014 OFC Women's Nations Cup to maintain her status as New Zealand's overall top scorer.

NETHERLANDS

ORANJE LEEUWINNEN SET TO MAKE THEIR WORLD BOW

The Netherlands had to play its heart out to make it to Canada 2015, competing not only in the qualifying group but in four high-pressure playoff matches. The players w savor its world bow, but how well can they expect to do this summer?

COACH

ROGER REIJNERS

A midfielder who won four caps for the Netherlands under-21s, Reijners spent his club career with professional teams Fortuna Sittard and MVV Maastricht. His playing career ended in 1995, but he went on to become first-team head coach at both of his former clubs. He followed the successful Vera Pauw as national women's team coach in November 2010 and is keen on possession-based soccer. The 51-year-old led the team through to qualification for the UEFA Women's Euro 2013 and the FIFA Women's World Cup 2015, with a contract in place until the Olympic Games in 2016.

The Dutch fared poorly in their last big tournament, the UEFA Women's Euro 2013. They finished bottom of a tough group, a disappointing showing after having reached the last four of the competition in 2009, their first outing in a major finals. They bounced back in November 2014, however, when they concluded an impressive FIFA Women's World Cup qualification campaign with a guaranteed place in the finals and their confidence on the big stage restored.

"After the last European Championship we discussed what we wanted and what we needed to improve," said head coach Roger Reijners. "And you see that we really have taken steps since the beginning of this year."

Indeed, with such a strong defense, creative midfield, and clinical attack, they might even go on to spring a few surpris in Canada. Reijners's players, who mostl compete in the BeNe League that featur teams from Belgium and the Netherland certainly showed a steely resolve to take Europe's best in their bid to reach the FI tournament in the Land of the Maple Le All told, group champion Norway was th only team to beat them during their lon qualification campaign, and in the final a mere two points were all that separate the two.

Second was not enough to automatic qualify for Canada, but the Dutch were

They may have booked their place to th party later than most, but the Dutch wil be raring to go come June.

KEY PLAYER

VIVIANNE MIEDEMA
Born: July 15, 1996

Described by coaches and media alike as a "phenomenon," this 18-year-old is one of the hottest prospects in Europe. Making her senior debut as a substitute against Albania in the first of the Netherlands' FIFA Women's World Cup qualification matches, she went on to top score with 16 goals in the campaign. Miedema has two great feet and can turn even half-chances into goals, but her celebrations can be remarkably understated. She spearheaded the Netherlands' first major women's title triumph, the 2014 UEFA European Women's Under-19 Championship, and was named the tournament's Golden Player after scoring six goals. She is the highest scorer in the BeNe League in 2014 with sc Heerenveen and joined German Frauen-Bundesliga club FC Bayern Munich that summer.

WORLD CUP RECORD

The Dutch defeated Scotland and Italy in the UEFA playoffs, played over two legs each, to bag a place at its first ever FIFA Women's World Cup.

ong the four best runners-up, and y maintained their momentum in the yoffs that followed. Scotland was beaten ne and away to set up two do-or-die ounters with Italy. "It's about playing he World Cup for the first time ever," record goalscorer Manon Melis. "It

will be all or nothing." Dutch teenager Vivianne Miedema certainly gave the matches all she had, and her three goals in both, resulting in a 1–1 draw in front of 13,100 at Den Haag and a 2–1 win in the return in Verona, were enough to see the Netherlands through.

It will have pleased the Dutch that Miedema was so instrumental in their historic feat. The teenager was key to the Netherlands' victory in the UEFA European Women's Under-19 Championship in 2014, and that crown bodes well for this nation's future prospects. The Netherlands today are strong, physical, and soccer savvy. With the UEFA Women's Euro due to take place in the Netherlands in 2017, the eyes of the world are on this ever-improving women's soccer nation.

LOOK OUT FOR

OES GEURTS
orn: January 12, 1986
osition: Goalkeeper

eurts became first choice in 2006 fter the retirement of record cap older Marleen Wissink. Now the rock t the heart of the Dutch defense, she a calm and organizing influence. An ble shot-stopper who is brave and ffective in one-on-ones, she eveloped her skills as a child against er brothers, using a bus shelter for a oal! She won Eredivisie Vrouwen tles with AZ Alkmaar before playing Sweden's Damallsvenskan with ittsjo GIK and Goteborg FC.

LIEKE MARTENS
Born: December 16, 1992
Position: Forward

Martens is a technically smart right-footed player with power and pace who most often operates on the left side. She has played for sc Heerenveen and VVV-Venlo in the Dutch Eredivisie Vrouwen and for Standard de Liege in the Belgian Women's Elite League, scoring as they won the BeNe SuperCup two years in a row. She has also played in Germany with FCR 2001 Duisburg and for Goteborg FC of the Swedish Damallsvenskan.

MANON MELIS
Born: August 31, 1986
Position: Forward

Daughter of former Feyenoord and Den Haag attacker Harry, Melis is one of the fastest players in the women's game, a clinical finisher, and a reliable goal scorer with more than a century of caps and counting. Melis has also shown her world-class credentials at club level in the highly competitive Swedish Damallsvenskan, topping the scoring charts three times, winning three titles, and claiming individual accolades during spells with LdB FC Malmo and Goteborg FC.

The rejuvenated Lansdowne Stadium is home to Ottawa Fury FC of the North American Soccer League.

ROUP B

wo newcomers and two old foes combine here,
nd while all the games will be watched eagerly,
nticipation is split between waiting to see who will
ome out on top on June 11 when Germany faces
orway in Ottawa, and when Côte d'Ivoire and
hailand meet there just hours later.

GERMANY
GIANTS OF THE GAME GO FOR GOLD

Germany is an ever-present team in the FIFA Women's World Cup. One of only four nations to have lifted the trophy in its 24-year history, it has won the tournament twice. Could Germany make it a trio of titles in 2015?

COACH

SILVIA NEID

Former midfielder Neid enjoyed a glittering career as a player, winning a host of league and cup titles and captaining Germany to European glory in 1989, scoring as it retained the title two years later. She was assistant to successful Germany coach Tina Theune from 1996 to 2005 and also coached at the youth level, winning several UEFA and FIFA tournaments with the under-18s and -19s. She took over the senior side in 2005. A runner-up in the FIFA Women's World Cup as a player, she won the competition as Germany's coach in 2007 and has overseen two UEFA Women's Euro title triumphs. Neid has been crowned world coach of the year by FIFA and values honesty and discipline in her work.

There is every chance the team may do, given a sumptuous qualification campaign that saw it record a perfect 10 out of 10 victories. A remarkable 62 goals were scored, with just four conceded, and Germany's ticket to Canada was in the bag with a game to spare—it went on to finish eight points clear of second-placed Russia in September 2014.

Sandwiched inside that brilliant campaign was an Algarve Cup triumph in March 2014, which included a 3–0 win in the final over FIFA Women's World Cup holders Japan. Ironically, the Nadeshiko had ejected Germany from the FIFA Women's World Cup 2011 at the quarterfinal stage, a knockout on home soil that shocked onlookers and dashed its hopes of qualification for the London 2012 Olympic Games.

There is little doubt that Silvia Neid's Germany is a different prospect these da Given its recent run, the group we can expect to see in Canada is ripe for succe The first glimpse of the team's promise came in the UEFA Women's Euro 2013 in Sweden, when injuries to key players me that Neid needed to revamp her squad. A string of up-and-coming starlets such as Nadine Kessler and Dzsenifer Marozsan came into the fray, and although they we far from imperious in the group stages, went on to make the final.

Often one of the most impressive things about any German team is not just the caliber of the starting eleven but also the quality of those players waiting in the win

KEY PLAYER

ANJA MITTAG
Born: May 16, 1985

Mittag is the spearhead of the German attack who can play wide or operate in the number 10 role; she bagged the winning goal in the UEFA Women's Euro 2013 final and top-scored for Germany in FIFA Women's World Cup qualification with 11 in nine matches. Also on target, she helped Germany beat Japan in the Algarve Cup final. A Golden Player in the 2004 UEFA European Women's Under-19 Championship, she was a member of Germany's FIFA Women's World Cup 2007 winning side. She suffered a dip by her own standards, but since joining LdB FC Malmo (now FC Rosengard) in the Swedish Damallsvenskan in 2012, she has roared back to form and was crowned league player, and top scorer of that year and again in 2014.

...here, they beat Norway 1–0. thanks ...a blistering goal from substitute Anja ...tag, although veteran keeper and ...ntual UEFA Player of the Tournament ...dine Angerer had to make two crucial ...alty saves to secure that eighth ...rman Euro title.

The majority of that squad went on to pass their next big test—qualification for the FIFA Women's World Cup—prompting Neid to praise the tightness of the group. "We have a lot of strength in depth and we work well together," she said.

WORLD CUP RECORD

Year	Venue	Result
1991	China	Fourth place
1995	Sweden	Runner-up
1999	USA	Quarterfinalists
2003	USA	Winners
2007	China	Winners
2011	Germany	Quarterfinalists

Given the players at Germany's disposal, and, with FIFA U-20 Women's World Cup winners Sara Dabritz, Pauline Bremer, and Lena Petermann knocking on the door, Neid does indeed have strength in depth. That, coupled with the impetus that a technically, tactically, and physically competitive domestic league, such as the Frauen-Bundesliga, can offer a solid national team, suggests that this Germany could come of age in Canada.

LOOK OUT FOR

EONIE MAIER
Born: September 29, 1992
Position: Defender

...ugely accomplished, Maier is an ...verlapping fullback who shone for ...ermany on its way to UEFA Women's ...uro gold in 2013 despite having only ...ade her senior debut in February of ...hat year. She has solid experience of ...ournament play at the youth level, ...inning the UEFA European Women's ...hampionship with the under-17s in ...009 and the under-19s in 2011 before ...aking silver at the FIFA U-20 Women's ...orld Cup 2012. Suffering an anterior ...ruciate ligament injury in March 2014, ...he gallantly battled back to play for ...C Bayern Munich by October.

NADINE KESSLER
Born: April 4, 1988
Position: Midfielder

Crowned FIFA and UEFA best women's player in Europe in 2014—and not without reason—Kessler is determined and creative, a genuine playmaker and natural striker of the ball who can carve goals out of nothing. A star in the underage groups, she was a captain with the under-19s and debuted for the seniors in 2010. A key member of the 2013 UEFA Women's Euro-winning squad, she won the UEFA Women's Champions League with 1. FFC Turbine Potsdam (and Anja Mittag) and as a captain with VfL Wolfsburg.

DZSENIFER MAROZSAN
Born: April 18, 1992
Position: Midfielder

One of the most talented players of her generation, Marozsan boasts super skills, great control, and accurate dead-ball delivery. She played her part in the 2013 UEFA Women's Euro tournament victory, scoring in the 1–0 semifinal win over Sweden. She hails from soccer stock; her father played for Hungary. She won the Golden Shoe and Silver Ball in the FIFA U-17 Women's World Cup in 2008, along with the Golden Ball in the U-20 edition in 2012. She is the youngest player to debut in the Frauen-Bundesliga with 1. FC Saarbrucken at age 14, seven months.

CÔTE D'IVOIRE
DEBUT NATION HAS WHAT IT TAKES TO IMPRESS THE WORLD

Côte d'Ivoire may have been the surprise package of its FIFA Women's World Cup qualifying tournament in Namibia, but its potential was there for all to see. Now the world waits to see if these gifted debut players can spring yet more surprises in Canada

COACH

CLEMENTINE TOURE

The 38-year-old was part of the coaching team that steered Equatorial Guinea to the African Women's Championship title in 2008. As head coach of her home nation she ironically saw her charges eliminate Equatorial Guinea on their way to qualification for the continental finals in 2014. She was one of three women coaches at the tournament proper—a first for the championship—and is very much a role model in the women's game in Africa. She made history when her team qualified for the FIFA Women's World Cup 2015—and her tactical awareness was seen as a key component of that achievement.

The teams that are drawn against this West African team this summer will most definitely need to be on their toes—Les Elephantes have more than just technique in their lockers. Observers at their FIFA Women's World Cup qualifying competition, the African Women's Championship, trumpeted their movement, positional awareness, dogged determination, and defensive sensibility, too. And as even the best teams in the world know, opponents with such an array of abilities in their armory can sometimes be the trickiest customers to overcome on the big stage, regardless of their history in the tournament.

Refreshingly for head coach Clementine Toure, the team that arrives in Canada will have no tournament backstory to live up to or put behind them because Côte d'Ivoire has never before qualified for a FIFA women's competition—at any level. So while these slight but sprightly players will have the steepest of learning curves to climb in Canada, they have nothing to prove and everything to gain, and so should play with freedom, joy, and pride. They ought to be confident, too, after having reached Canada 2015 thanks to some promising displays in the African Women's Championship.

Having comfortably overcome Mali and then defending champions Equatorial

With all to play for and little to lose, Les Elephantes will learn a lot from their debut in Canada.

KEY PLAYER

ESTELLE JOSEE NAHI
Born: May 29, 1989

An inspirational captain who can play on the wing or lead the line, Nahi has the playing sensibility and technique to be a genuine game-changer—as she showed in the qualifying competition for Canada 2015, the African Women's Championship in Namibia. She scored 13 minutes into her first game in the competition, and went on to set up chances for others and score again as Côte d'Ivoire ultimately bagged the third African place on offer. She has experience playing in the UEFA Women's Champions League with Serbian outfit Spartak Subotica and Russian team WFC Zvezda 2005, finding the back of the net for both clubs while representing them in the elite European competition. Nahi will relish the chance to play against the best in the world.

WORLD CUP RECORD

Finishing third at only its second African Women's Championship was enough to see Côte d'Ivoire make its debut at the finals in Canada.

...nea in the preliminary rounds to qualify ...the championship, the team got off to ...icky start in the competition proper ...Namibia in October 2014. Opening ...h a 4–2 loss to eventual winners (for ...ecord seventh time) Nigeria was a ...back, but the Ivorians, who were making ...y their second-ever appearance at

the championship, went on to beat host Namibia and draw with Zambia before losing in extra time to experienced African Women's Championship outfit Cameroon in the semifinal.

With Africa receiving three qualifying places at the FIFA Women's World Cup for the first time, however, there was still much

to play for as Les Elephantes went into the third-place playoff with South Africa. Little wonder then that head coach Toure was mobbed by her joyous players after Ida Rebecca Guehai's 85th-minute goal secured victory over Banyana Banyana in Windhoek. It was a historic win, and the victory not only booked Côte d'Ivoire a ticket to Canada—it also announced the country's potential as one of the top nations in African women's soccer.

LOOK OUT FOR

KOKO ANGE N'GUESSAN
Born: November 18, 1990
Position: Midfielder/Forward

Described by observers as "too hot to handle" during the African Women's Championship, N'Guessan combined with Nahi to pester opposition defenses. Light on her feet, speedy, and skillful, she is not the biggest member of the team, but she plays without fear and ran South Africa ragged down both flanks in the playoff for the third FIFA Women's World Cup 2015 spot. Capable of scoring in key games, she was crowned 2013 Ivorian Football Federation Player of the Year.

IDA REBECCA GUEHAI
Born: July 15, 1994
Position: Midfielder

Guehai is a goal-scoring midfielder who bagged the vital win in the African Women's Championship match against South Africa that booked her nation's place in its first-ever FIFA Women's World Cup. She also captained the under-20s in their bid to qualify for the FIFA U-20 Women's World Cup 2014. Recognized as one of the best players in Côte d'Ivoire's Championnat National Féminin, she top-scored in 2014 and was named Ivorian Football Federation Player of the Year.

TIA INES N'REHY
Born: October 1, 1993
Position: Forward

An instinctive striker with fine, close control and aerial ability, N'Rehy was Côte d'Ivoire's leading scorer in its FIFA Women's World Cup 2015 qualifying campaign, with three goals. With loads of energy, she is an important cog in her nation's fluid attacking line. Another player with UEFA Women's Champions League experience, she scored during her debut in the league for Serbian team Spartak Subotica in 2013, hitting a hat trick in the qualifiers in 2014.

NORWAY

PROUD WOMEN'S SOCCER NATION LOOKS BACK TO THE FUTU

Norway was a happy victor when it lifted the FIFA Women's World Cup trophy in Sweden in 1995. Twenty years on, the world wonders if history could repeat itself, th time in Canada.

COACH

EVEN PELLERUD

A great character in the game, he boasts more than 40 years' experience, having played and coached in the Norwegian men's top flight—and a good deal of success, too, with his trademark style of direct soccer. He enjoyed immense triumphs with Norway in the 1990s, during which time he led the team to the FIFA Women's World Cup and UEFA Women's Euro gold. He took Canada to two FIFA Women's World Cups and won the Cyprus Cup with the Canucks in 2008. He coached Trinidad and Tobago for four years before returning to Norway for a second spell. Now in his 60s, he remains one of soccer's most energetic figures, and the players say he has reinvigorated the squad.

The Grasshoppers will give it everything they have got—and that is quite a lot if you run the rule over their roster of exciting players and consider the pedigree of the coach who led them to qualification for 2015. Even Pellerud was at the helm when Norway achieved FIFA Women's World Cup glory in 1995, and since his return to the national setup in 2012 he has shown his expertise yet again.

Pellerud has mixed precocious youngsters, such as the attack-minded Caroline Graham Hansen and Ada Stolsmo Hegerberg, in with experienced heads like keeper Ingrid Hjelmseth and defensive midfielder Maren Mjelde to create a vibrant, competitive, and cohesive Norway.

In the summer of 2013 the team put in a stellar performance in the UEFA Women Euro in Sweden, going all the way to th final, where it pushed Germany to the limit before losing 1–0 after having two penalties saved.

The team then brushed itself off from disappointment to put in a fine qualifyin campaign for the FIFA Women's World C eventually beating the Netherlands to fi place in Group 5. Norway lost just once along the way, and that was in its final match, at home to the Netherlands four days after the team had already booked tickets, thanks to an 11–0 whitewash of

Norwegian women's teams always have fighting spirit and little fear. The youngst are not lacking in craft either.

KEY PLAYER

CAROLINE GRAHAM HANSEN
Born: February 18, 1995

A standout player of the women's game, the midfielder/forward has been labeled fearless, exciting, and mature by seasoned observers. Still only 20 years old, she boasts amazing control and can cause mayhem in any back line with her speedy dribbling and fierce runs. She was part of Norway's 2011 UEFA European Women's Under-19 Championship silver-medal-winning side and debuted for the seniors that year. She went into the UEFA Women's Euro 2013 with just 16 caps, but turned into one of its major players as Norway finished runner-up. A Norwegian league winner with Stabaek when she was just 15, she was snapped up by Tyreso FF of Sweden in 2013 and joined German side VfL Wolfsburg in 2014, experiencing valuable UEFA Women's Champions League competition with all three clubs.

WORLD CUP RECORD

Year	Venue	Result
1991	China	Runner-up
1995	Sweden	Winners
1999	USA	Fourth place
2003	USA	Quarterfinalists
2007	China	Fourth place
2011	Germany	Group stage (3rd, Group D)

...bania away in Durres.

...ellerud, a veteran of four FIFA Women's ...orld Cups, was delighted to have steered ...eam to a fifth, describing the feeling ...qualification as "fantastic." "We are ...nfirmed as finals contenders," he added.

"That's phenomenal."

What perhaps is more remarkable is the way that Norway has come back into contention since its team, hit by injury, did the unthinkable and crashed out of the FIFA Women's World Cup 2011 at the group stage. Almost half of that 2011 squad remain, and many played their part in Norway's success at the Women's Euro 2013 and in the FIFA Women's World Cup qualification; the new faces have played beyond their years in both.

All will have learned from their experiences, and though a disappointingly low finish in the 2014 Algarve Cup suggests there is still work to be done, the foundations are there for Norway to become great again.

LOOK OUT FOR

INGRID HJELMSETH
Born: April 10, 1980
Position: Goalkeeper

A great communicator and brilliant distributor, this qualified software engineer is the safest of hands. Debuting in 2003, Hjelmseth has been number 1 since 2009. Part of the Norway squad that finished second at the UEFA Women's Euro 2005 and third place four years later, she was named to the all-star UEFA Women's Euro 2013 squad and was vital to qualifying for Canada. She has won multiple domestic titles with SK Trondheims-Orn and Stabaek, and in 2013 she was named the Golden Ball winner by the Norwegian Football Association.

MAREN MJELDE
Born: November 6, 1989
Position: Defender/Midfielder

A solid defensive midfielder, Mjelde has turned in many strong performances at center-back for her country, but she was also a revelation at right fullback in the UEFA Women's Euro 2013, deservedly making the All-Star squad. She has experience captaining teams in UEFA and FIFA youth tournaments and is a born leader. Hailing from a soccer-playing family (brother Erik is a professional), she played UEFA Women's Champions League soccer with 1. FFC Turbine Potsdam before moving to Sweden's Damallsvenskan.

ADA STOLSMO HEGERBERG
Born: July 10, 1995
Position: Forward

A striker with an eye for the spectacular as well as the speculative, Hegerberg has great technique and sees and tries things that other players do not and dare not. Part of an exciting new generation, she debuted for the seniors in 2011 and was still a student during Norway's exciting run to the final of the UEFA Women's Euro 2013. Norwegian Players' Association young player of the year in 2011, she joined German outfit 1. FFC Turbine Potsdam in 2013 and then France's Olympique Lyonnais in 2014.

THAILAND

HISTORY MAKERS GEAR UP TO NEXT MILESTONE

Thailand has the honor of becoming the first Southeast Asian country to qualify for a FIFA Women's World Cup. A relatively unknown quantity, its participation will be watched with interest.

COACH

NUENGRUETHAI SATHONGWIEN

A double history-maker—Sathongwien is the first woman to lead the national team and in 2014 became the first to lead any Thai team to a senior FIFA World Cup tournament. A graduate of the Faculty of Sports Science of Kasetsart University, she was in charge of the Thai Women's Premier League side BG-CAS. She joined the national team as assistant coach in 2013 before taking over the reins in the lead-up to the AFC Women's Asian Cup. She is also responsible for the youth setup. She cites the team's qualification for Canada 2015 as a significant moment for the women's game in Thailand.

Not that this will be anything new to Thailand—the team played the must-win AFC Women's Asian Cup match that secured its qualifying spot for Canada 2015 in front of a reported 18,000 fans on its rivals' home turf.

Success in the AFC Women's Asian Cup has secured the FIFA Women's World Cup places of five teams from the Asian confederation. Heading into the tournament in May 2014, Thailand was one of the favorites to clinch a place.

The Thais had won their group in the preliminary round, although they were tested to the limit by the Philippines. And they came into the cup competition having won gold for the fifth time in their history during the Southeast Asian Games the previous December, beating near neighbo Vietnam 2–1.

Once the AFC Women's Asian Cup kick off, Thailand knew it would have to deal with the ambitions of fellow Group B sid Myanmar and the more experienced Kore Republic and China PR to keep its own Fl Women's World Cup dreams alive.

It was a tough ask, and Korea and China both got the better of head coach Nuengruethai Sathongwien's charges, w were unable to get a goal against their opponents in two high-scoring matches.

Midfielder Kanjana Sung-Ngoen and

No women's side from Thailand has reach a senior FIFA finals, so this is new territor for the team and the soccer-watching wo

KEY PLAYER

KANJANA SUNG-NGOEN
Born: September 21, 1986

She likes to patrol the right flank of the Thailand midfield, but with her blistering pace, Sung-Ngoen can complement the front line, scoring goals and setting up her teammates with unselfish passes or a pinpoint dead-ball delivery. She has won gold with Thailand in the Southeast Asian Games and scored the two goals against Vietnam in the AFC Women's Asian Cup that booked its place in Canada; she also scored in the final of the ASEAN Football Federation Women's Championship to help Thailand win the tournament for the first time in 2011. She won rave reviews from spectators for her speed and skill during a spell in Japan with Nadeshiko League team Speranza FC in 2013.

WORLD CUP RECORD

Newcomer Thailand is also the first team from the Southeast Asian region ever to qualify for a FIFA Women's World Cup finals.

The team passed with flying colors as Kanjana Sung-Ngoen again found the target with a brace in the second half to seal a 2–1 win over Vietnam in a vibrant Thong Nhat Stadium in Ho Chi Minh City.

"This victory, and thereby qualifying for the World Cup, is a very important milestone in our development," declared coach Sathongwien afterward.

The coach was right. Thailand had written its name into FIFA Women's World Cup history—and now the world awaits their next chapter.

ender Sritala Duangnapa both found the : for Thailand against Myanmar, though, the Thais edged the match 2–1 to sh third in their group.

hat crucial placing meant that if they ld beat the third-place team in Group they would still qualify for the FIFA Women's World Cup.

Given that the team Thailand was due to face was Vietnam, who was both competition host and the outfit Thailand had recently seen off in its quest to win gold in the Southeast Asian Games, this would undoubtedly be a test of nerves for Thailand.

LOOK OUT FOR

ARUT CHANGPLOOK
Born: February 3, 1988
Position: Defender

Another player who has enjoyed gold medal success in the ASEAN Football Federation Women's Championship and Southeast Asian Games, Changplook played every minute of the AFC Women's Asian Cup to help Thailand qualify for Canada 2015. Easily spotted on the pitch with her dyed hair, she is a joy to watch and is capable of playing across the back line or in midfield, according to the flow of the game. She has the composure and skill to instigate attacks, and she likes to shoot when the chance arises.

TANEEKARN DANGDA
Born: December 15, 1992
Position: Forward

Dangda was part of the Thailand team that won gold in the Southeast Asian Games in December 2013. One of the tallest players in the Thailand squad, the 22-year-old gained valuable experience playing with Swedish team Ostersunds DFF during its promotion-chasing season of 2014 as part of a player exchange program. She follows in the footsteps of her brother Teerasil, who has come up through the ranks of the Thai men's national team.

NISA ROMYEN
Born: January 18, 1990
Position: Forward

A consistent goalscorer for her country at both youth and senior levels, Romyen instinctively hits the target and is at her most dangerous from close range. Romyen can grab a goal with her head or feet and was top scorer in the 2014 Asian Games. She hit eight goals to help Thailand in the preliminary rounds of the FIFA Women's World Cup qualifying competition, the AFC Women's Asian Cup, and played in every match as Thailand went on to secure a place in Canada.

BC Place in Vancouver, the main stadium for the 2010 Winter Olympics, is the venue for the final of the FIFA Women's World Cup 2015.

GROUP C

ere, current title holders Japan are pitted against
ree debut teams. It seems a foregone conclusion
at the Nadeshiko will emerge in pole position, but
e book could still be rewritten, and the opening
wo fixtures may indicate whether Switzerland,
ameroon, or Ecuador are strong enough to
allenge the champions.

JAPAN
CAN THE NADESHIKO RETAIN THEIR CROWN?

Japan lit up the sport in 2011 when it beat the USA in a thrill-a-minute final to becom[e] the first Asian team to win a senior World Cup. Will the team have us all on our feet again in 2015?

COACH

NORIO SASAKI

Sasaki played for NTT Kanto Soccer Club and retired from the game in his early 30s. He coached men early on in his career but joined Japan's women's structure as a youth coach in 2006. Taking charge of the seniors in 2007, he first tasted success in the 2008 East Asian championship and the Olympics. He was named FIFA women's soccer coach of the year in 2011— justifiably so, given Japan's World Cup–winning performance in Germany that year—and went on to lead the Nadeshiko to silver in the London 2012 Olympics. He is known as a tough trainer with a sense of humor, a style that has paid off in spades thus far.

Humble, fast, and dynamic, Japan certainly surprised the world with its refusal to lie down in the face of one of the greatest women's soccer-playing nations.

Since that unforgettable FIFA Women's World Cup night in a sold-out stadium in Frankfurt in July 2011, Japan has gone on to claim its first-ever Olympic silver medal and its maiden AFC Women's Asian Cup title.

The team was disappointed to lose its Asian Games title to Korea DPR in October 2014, but the Japanese knew they had at least secured the chance to defend its FIFA Women's World Cup title when they won in Asia in May. Topping their AFC Women's Asian Cup group secured their qualification for Canada, and they went on to beat rivals

China PR and Australia to claim the crown[.]

It seems remarkable now that Japan had not won the AFC Women's Asian Cup in its history until 2014, but it is perhaps a sign [of] how tight competition is between the tea[ms] in the confederation.

The nation's wins over China and Australi[a] were certainly narrow—a single goal decid[ed] both games, with defender Azusa Iwashimi[zu] goals proving crucial in both matches.

Japan was without key names in the tournament, however, with club commitments depriving them of players o[f] the caliber of defender Yukari Kinga and

Coach Norio Sasaki likes to rotate his starting lineups; this team faced Korea D[PR] in the sixth East Asian Games.

KEY PLAYER

AYA MIYAMA
Born: January 28, 1985

As the captain, Miyama is a set-piece specialist with a dangerous right foot. She can boss a match with her vision and skill and is regularly hailed for her ability to think on her feet as well as her stamina and agility; she always puts in a shift. A multiple Asian Player of the Year Award winner and all-star team member of the FIFA Women's World Cup 2011, she was so influential in the 2014 AFC Women's Asian Cup that she was named most valuable player of the tournament. Miyama practices her free kicks until they are perfect and says she is always thinking of set plays and how to improve them. She has played in the USA, returning to Okayama Yunogo Belle in Japan's Nadeshiko League in 2010. Quite simply, she is a world-class midfielder.

WORLD CUP RECORD

Year	Venue	Result
1991	China	Group stage (4th, Group B)
1995	Sweden	Quarterfinalists
1999	USA	Group stage (4th, Group C)
2003	USA	Group stage (3rd, Group C)
2007	China	Group stage (3rd, Group C)
2011	Germany	Winners

...acker Shinobu Ohno, who starred for ...glish team Arsenal in 2014.
...hat said, coach Norio Sasaki seized the ...ance to bring up-and-coming players into ...e fray in Vietnam, with former underage ...rlets Chinatsu Kira, Hikaru Naomoto, and ...ka Norimatsu getting their feet wet.

Sasaki said one of his tasks in the run-up to Canada was to blend Japan's young prospects with established performers. One of the latter members of that elite group is striker Yuki Ogimi, a FIFA Women's World Cup winner who has strengthened her game by playing in Europe. "We are not satisfied

just to have qualified because the goal is to win the tournament," she said. "And we want to show you our football and make you enjoy yourself!"

Fans everywhere will surely do that this summer when Japan once again showcases its skills on the world stage, this time on Canadian soil.

LOOK OUT FOR

AZUSA IWASHIMIZU
Born: October 14, 1986
Position: Defender

Comfortable in possession, brave, and strong, Iwashimizu debuted on the senior team in 2006 and went on to feature in the FIFA Women's World Cup in 2007 and 2011. She was sent off in the last minute as Japan won the competition for the first time in 2011. She loves to go up for set pieces and grab a goal, as does her defensive partner Saki Kumagai, with whom she has a great understanding. She scored two crucial goals to see Japan to victory in the AFC Women's Asian Cup.

HOMARE SAWA
Born: September 6, 1978
Position: Midfielder

Sawa scored five goals and set up another as she carried Japan to a famous victory in the FIFA Women's World Cup 2011, her fifth finals appearance. She also won the tournament's Golden Ball and Boot, and went on to be crowned FIFA Women's World Player of the Year. Composed and extremely experienced, this 36-year-old veteran is a big game player who continues to play her part, competing in the final as Japan lifted its first-ever AFC Women's Asian Cup in 2014.

MANA IWABUCHI
Born: March 18, 1993
Position: Forward

This diminutive striker is a big hitter on the pitch, with a breathtaking touch and sublime skill. Arriving on the international scene as a teenager in the FIFA U-17 Women's World Cup 2008, Iwabuchi was crowned the tournament's Golden Ball and then AFC Women's Youth Player of the Year. Part of the FIFA Women's World Cup 2011 title-winning team, she has honed her talent by playing in Germany and joined Bayern Munich in 2014. She is a great role model for any young player.

SWITZERLAND

A DEBUT TEAM LOOKS TO MAKE AN IMPACT

Switzerland is among the debut nations at this expanded FIFA Women's World Cup, and the first European team to qualify. Will it maintain its winning ways in Canada?

COACH

MARTINA VOSS-TECKLENBURG

A former German international, 47-year-old Voss-Tecklenburg knows a thing or two about soccer. A veteran of three FIFA Women's World Cups and a four-time Euro winner, she was an attacking midfielder/forward with 125 caps for her country. She also won a host of titles as a player with TSV Siegen and went on to taste success as a coach when she guided FCR 2001 Duisburg to two German cups and victory in the UEFA Women's Cup 2009. She worked as editor-in-chief of German women's soccer magazine *FF* for five years. In 2012 she joined Switzerland after a brief stint with FF USV Jena and has instilled a winning mentality, overseeing an unbeaten qualifying campaign.

The Swiss would like to think so, particularly when they look back at a blistering qualification campaign. Iceland, Israel, Serbia, Malta, and UEFA Women's Euro 2013 semifinalists Denmark all had to be overcome on the road to Canada.

Switzerland made light work of these obstacles, conceding just one goal and hitting an impressive 53 past its group rivals, including 16 on aggregate against both Serbia and Malta.

Its 9–0 obliteration of Israel in June 2014, coupled with a 1–1 draw between Denmark and Iceland the following day, confirmed Switzerland's qualification with two games to spare.

"No one could have expected us to go through so easily," said head coach Martina Voss-Tecklenburg after she and squad had followed the stalemate betwe Denmark and Iceland on the Internet wit eager anticipation.

Switzerland continued to make it look easy with two further victories, concludir its campaign unbeaten and nine points clear of nearest rivals Iceland.

Of course, the Swiss surprised onlooker in the qualifiers for the 2011 edition of the FIFA Women's World Cup, too. They topped their group but missed out in tha tournament's playoffs.

When coach Beatrice von Siebenthal

Switzerland cruised toward Canada in qualifying; they will be ready to kick off against Japan in Vancouver.

KEY PLAYER

RAMONA BACHMANN
Born: December 25, 1990

She has been dubbed the "Swiss Magician" and first stunned Europe in 2009 when she unveiled her bag of tricks in the UEFA European Women's Under-19 Championship. Named Golden Player of that tournament, Bachmann was also voted Swiss player of the year in 2009. A precocious talent, the 24-year-old striker is skillful and strong, and few can rival her killer touch in front of goal. She was signed for Umea IK in the Swedish Damallsvenskan at the age of 16 and went on to play for Atlanta Beat in the Women's Professional Soccer league in America, as well as Swedish champions LdB FC Malmo (now known as FC Rosengard). Voted Damallsvenskan player of the year in 2011 and 2013, the Swiss number 10 is a definite crowd-pleaser.

WORLD CUP RECORD

No more playoffs or repechage disappointment for the Swiss, who made no mistakes this time around. This will be their first finals appearance.

...pped down, she left a team capable of ...king it with the best in Europe, and the ...ti have kicked on since Voss-Tecklenburg ...k the reins in January 2012. An advocate of solidity in defense while ...king the most of a wealth of attacking ...ent, the former German international is ...en on creativity, courage, and confidence.

The Swiss have that in spades, particularly in midfielder Lara Dickenmann and strikers Ana Maria Crnogorcevic and Ramona Bachmann, who have experience playing league soccer in France, Germany, and Sweden, respectively.

They are not alone; several Swiss seniors make their living in competitive leagues outside their home country, and that on-field experience is paying off for the national team. As is the know-how that some of Voss-Tecklenburg's squad will have picked up both in a string of FIFA U-20 Women's World Cup finals appearances and at Switzerland's national academy, which gives the best young players a chance to combine soccer with study.

Having finally reached a major senior tournament, the Swiss now have a chance to teach the world how far this small nation has come.

LOOK OUT FOR

NOELLE MARITZ
Born: December 23, 1995
Position: Defender

Cool, strong, and quick, 19-year-old Maritz was born in America and grew up playing soccer and baseball. She competed in mixed teams and can mix it with the strongest opponents. She made the first-team squad at FC Zurich at just age 15 and was signed by German giants VfL Wolfsburg in 2013. Maritz represented Switzerland in major tournaments at the youth level before making her senior debut in 2013. She featured in every Switzerland game in the qualifiers.

LIA WALTI
Born: April 19, 1993
Position: Midfielder

A former Young Boys star, this versatile player can hold her own in center-midfield, left wing, or even left-back. A fine ball crosser, Walti played in the UEFA Women's Champions League with Young Boys and was snapped up by German Frauen-Bundesliga powerhouse 1. FFC Turbine Potsdam in 2013. She starred for Switzerland in the underage groups before joining the senior team, playing a large part in the qualifying campaign for Canada. She will relish her chance on the big stage.

LARA DICKENMANN
Born: November 27, 1985
Position: Midfielder

Five-time Swiss player of the year, 29-year-old Dickenmann can play through the middle or on the left, where her speed and directness can be devastatingly effective. Capable of goals that will take your breath away, she scored on her debut for the senior team at age 16. She played soccer in America at both the college and W-League level. She joined Olympique Lyonnais in 2008, where she has won the UEFA Women's Champions League and a string of French titles.

CAMEROON

LIONESSES LOOK TO BUILD ON OLYMPIC LESSONS

Cameroon was described as a "powerhouse" team on its way to qualification for Canada 2015. Will they be too strong for the top teams to handle in Canada? The Indomitable Lionesses will certainly offer every team they encounter a tough test.

COACH

CARL ENOW NGACHU

A former player and physical education teacher, the experienced 40-year-old coach has worked with Cameroon's national women's teams for more than a decade, at both youth and senior levels. He has rebuilt the Indomitable Lionesses squad to create a heady mix of experience and youth. He took Cameroon to victory in the All Africa Games in 2011 and secured a place at the London 2012 Olympics. Although they fared poorly in the latter competition, he remained upbeat and optimistic about their future. His confidence was rewarded in October 2014 when Cameroon qualified for its first-ever FIFA Women's World Cup.

They will relish their chance to do so, too—the Lionesses have gradually developed since their maiden competition outing 24 years ago, and this is the first time they have qualified for a FIFA Women's World Cup. That is not to say that Cameroon is short on tournament experience; it has plenty on its own continent and is an almost perennial semifinalist in the African Women's Championship.

Under head coach Carl Enow Ngachu, the Lionesses have kicked on even more in recent years, however, and in 2011 Cameroon was crowned champions at the All Africa Games in Mozambique without conceding a goal. In 2012 it got the chance to impose itself on the world when it became one of only three African teams to compete at a Women's Olympic Football Tournament. Losses in the London 2012 Olympics to host Great Britain as well as Brazil and New Zealand were chastening though probably not surprising, given that women's soccer in Cameroon is still a wo in progress.

Ngachu was determined that his young and spirited team should learn from its Olympic experience, though, and it will g the chance to show the world how far it has come at Canada 2015. "We are look forward to having an impact," Ngachu sa after his group qualified for this summer"

These tough cookies from Cameroon will relish the chance to compete against two fellow debut teams.

KEY PLAYER

GAELLE ENGANAMOUIT
Born: June 9, 1992

Tall, strong, and speedy, Enganamouit is the spearhead of Cameroon's front line. She started playing soccer with her brothers at the age of five and has a lifelong passion for the game. She was part of Cameroon's All Africa Games winning squad in 2011, scoring in the semifinal win over South Africa, and was also on the squad for the London 2012 Olympics. She played a key role in Cameroon's qualification for Canada 2015, scoring three goals and winning Player of the Match plaudits, and has experience playing in Sweden's highly competitive Damallsvenskan after joining Eskilstuna United DFF from Spartak Subotica in Serbia. She has been described as one of Cameroon's precious gems because of her fine soccer brain, confidence under pressure, and attacking ability.

WORLD CUP RECORD

Cameroon's runner-up spot at the African Women's Championship ensured it continues to break new ground, earning a place at its first FIFA Women's World Cup.

experience, and they are not the only members of the group testing their talent by playing in demanding leagues outside of Africa.

Many of the current squad have played in club soccer in Europe, and their experiences will undoubtedly help those youngsters in the group who continue to develop their game in clubs within Cameroon. These are heady days for this promising group. They have already shown their power and determination in Africa—now it is time for them to flex their soccer-playing muscle in front of the world.

A tournament by reaching the final of the African Women's Championship in October 2014.

Although favorite Nigeria went on to deny it the chance of lifting its first African Women's Championship title, Cameroon beat Namibia having impressed with its strength in defense, discipline in midfield, and liveliness in attack. Key to that hard-earned reputation were players such as goalkeeper of the tournament Annette Ngo Ndom, captain Christine Manie, and star striker Gaelle Enganamouit. All three boast UEFA Women's Champions League

LOOK OUT FOR

ANNETTE NGO NDOM
Born: June 2, 1985
Position: Goalkeeper

Ndom debuted on the national team in 2010 and a year later won gold at the All Africa Games in Mozambique. She is hailed for her brilliance in the victory over Nigeria that booked Cameroon's qualification for the London 2012 Olympics. She also played in the UEFA Women's Champions League with Slovakian team FC Union Nove Zamky. Named best keeper in the African Women's Championships in 2014, she was nominated for the 2014 African Women's Player of the Year award.

CHRISTINE MANIE
Born: May 4, 1984
Position: Defender

A composed defender who manages to pop up with crucial goals at key moments, Manie scored against Nigeria in the game that secured Cameroon's place at the London 2012 Olympics. The captain also headed home a late-late winner in the African Women's Championship semifinal against Côte d'Ivoire to guarantee her team a place in the FIFA Women's World Cup 2015. She has UEFA Women's Champions League experience with Romanian outfit Olimpia Cluj Napoca.

MADELEINE NGONO MANI
Born: October 16, 1983
Position: Forward

The team's speedy and superefficient goal machine and one of Cameroon's most popular players ever, Mani first came to prominence with Cameroonian clubs Lorema and Canon Yaounde. She has played for several teams in France, including Saint-Etienne, ASJ Soyaux, and Guingamp, and has a raft of tournament experience, scoring the winning goal for Cameroon when it won the 2011 All Africa Games. She has played every match of its historic qualification campaign for the FIFA Women's World Cup 2015.

ECUADOR
LA TRICOLOR EMBARKS ON ITS NEXT BIG ADVENTURE

When Ecuador learned of its opponents in the FIFA Women's World Cup 2015, the coach declared the team was set to experience an "amazing adventure." That much is true, although the journey to get there was pretty incredible, too.

COACH

VANESSA ARAUZ

The youngest coach in the history of any FIFA World Women's Cup tournament, Arauz will be just 26 when she leads La Tri at Canada 2015. Having joined Club Sport Emelec as a child, she went on to play for a regional select XI before becoming the first woman in Ecuador to qualify as a top-level coach. A dedicated scholar of the game, she undertook internships with professional men's clubs before joining La Tri as an assistant coach in 2011. Arauz stepped up to the main coaching role with the national team, as well as the youth squads, in March 2013.

That is because La Tri needed to stage a tremendous comeback to even stay in contention for FIFA Women's World Cup 2015 qualification and was then thrown into a last-gasp intercontinental playoff with Trinidad and Tobago to settle which of them would take the very last place on offer in Canada this summer.

Two automatic qualifying places and one intercontinental playoff qualification for Canada 2015 were on offer at the Copa America Femenina in September 2014, and after beating Peru and Venezuela in its group phase matches, host Ecuador joined Brazil, Colombia, and Argentina in the battle to clinch one of those spots.

A humbling 4–0 loss to As Canarinhas and 2–1 defeat at the hands of Las Cafeteras meant Ecuador needed to beat Argentina to finish third and reach the playoffs, but its dream looked in tatters when Las Albicelestes hit it with two early goals at Atahualpa Olympic Stadium in Quito. Ecuador was not finished, though, and it turned its motivational motto, "Nothing will stop us," into reality, rallying to turn around the tie and clinch the match 3–2. Its reward was another high-pressure game at the same venue a month later against Trinidad and Tobago, who had finished fourth in its own continental qualifiers.

Strong-willed and able, the newcomers from Ecuador could spring a surprise.

KEY PLAYER

ANDREA PESANTES
Born: January 14, 1988

A determined and energetic all-rounder (she also enjoys swimming and cycling) who was born in the Galapagos Islands, Pesantes played defense and midfield when younger, but is now the linchpin around whom Ecuador build its attacks. She has excellent close control, protects the ball well, especially in tight spaces, and has the confidence, energy, and technical ability to inspire her teammates in crucial matches. She represented her country at the South American Under-19 Women's Championship in 2004, at just age 16, and went on to play in Ecuador's first appearance at the Pan American Games. In 2013, she played in the inaugural season of the Ecuadorian national women's championship and won the title with Rocafuerte FC in 2014.

WORLD CUP RECORD

Ecuador was the last team to qualify for the finals—its debut at the competition—after defeating Trinidad and Tobago in an intercontinental playoff.

Women's soccer is still developing in Ecuador, but a new league is in place, and several members of the national team train every day with the 2014 champions Rocafuerte FC; a handful have even enjoyed silver medal success in the Bolivarian Games in 2009.

As it showed in its thrilling qualifying campaign, Ecuador is adaptable and determined. If it can show the same fight and ambition in Canada, we will all enjoy the team's next great adventure.

either side made the breakthrough in t first leg, the game finishing goalless, it was all to play for on December 2 in return in Port of Spain. It was Ecuador's t away match of its entire qualifying trail, d, spurred on by its "12th Warrior" fans at the Hasely Crawford Stadium, Trinidad and Tobago tested the visitors' defensive line time and again. The breakthrough, when it came, though, was Ecuador's, and the late-late winner from Monica Quinteros was a historic moment for her country.

LOOK OUT FOR

SHIRLEY BERRUZ
Born: January 6, 1991
Position: Goalkeeper

Berruz is a keeper with great agility and quick reflexes who was hailed as one of the heroines of La Tri's qualification for Canada after her raft of reaction stops in the playoff against Trinidad and Tobago. Having first tried soccer in her mid-teens, she was starting in goal for Ecuador before she hit 20. She received a pair of gloves from her hero, former national team goalkeeper Marcelo Elizaga, and was inspired to train even harder—dedication that is certainly paying off now.

LIGIA MOREIRA
Born: March 19, 1992
Position: Defender

This player has captained her club team and first wore the armband for La Tri in the lead-up to the Copa America Femenina. She was given the honor by coach Arauz, thanks to her strong character and leadership qualities at center-back as well as her calmness in possession and good distribution. Known as "Gigi" to her teammates, she first played soccer as a midfielder on a boys' team. A multiple title winner with Rocafuerte, she has also played in the Copa Libertadores Femenina.

MONICA QUINTEROS
Born: July 5, 1988
Position: Forward

Quinteros wrote her name into the history books after heading the goal in added time against Trinidad and Tobago that saw her team qualify for its first-ever FIFA Women's World Cup. A quick and powerful striker, the former Ecuador under-19 international hit 25 goals for Club 7 de Febrero in 2014. She missed the main qualifying tournament, the Copa America Femenina, on home soil due to her physical-education teaching commitments.

Opened in 2013, the stadium in Winnipeg is the newest of the venues for the FIFA Women's World Cup 2015.

GROUP D

here is no doubt that the D in this group is for eath! This is the fifth time Sweden and USA ave been drawn together at this stage, and he Americans have the edge with three wins. With Nigeria and Australia completing the heup, fans are in for a treat.

Group D

USA
TEAM USA CROSSES THE BORDER AS MAJOR CONTENDERS

Two-time FIFA Women's World Cup winner and losing finalists in the last edition of th[e] competition, the USA is always a strong favorite for the title. When the team arrives [in] Canada, those expectations will be as high as ever.

COACH

JILL ELLIS

A former college player, Ellis took the reins in the spring of 2014 following Tom Sermanni's departure. She has a long association with the national setup since being appointed to lead the under-21s in 2000 by then head coach April Heinrichs. She tasted gold-medal success while assistant to former USA coach Pia Sundhage at the 2008 and 2012 Olympics. Following her father, John, into coaching, she kicked off her own career with college teams including the UCLA Bruins, whom she led to a raft of titles. The 48-year-old is said to have coached nearly every player in the USA team pool at some stage— so she knows their myriad strengths— and will enjoy the challenges ahead.

That is not simply because the USA has always reached at least the semifinal stage of the elite world tournament; it is also because of the prowess it showed on the road to this 2015 edition.

The USA brushed aside all comers in the qualifying CONCACAF Women's Championship in October 2014, easing past Mexico 3–0 in the semifinal to book its place in Canada, before battering Costa Rica 6–0 in the final to win the trophy. That result brought its goal tally in the tournament to 21 without reply, an imperious vein of form made all the more impressive by the fact that new head coach Jill Ellis frequently switched around her starting lineup and their positions.

Only midfielder and eventual Golden Ball winner Carli Lloyd played all 450 minute[s] of the competition, but the fact that Elli[s] was still able to get the best out of ever[y] player illustrates both her qualities as a communicator and the determination of those on her roster to perform.

From center-back and captain Christie[e] Rampone, down to tricky players like Tobin Heath and Megan Rapinoe, and t[he] world's leading goalscorer Abby Wamb[ach] these are ominous opponents for any world team to encounter. And regardles[s] of which players make the final squad this summer, the majority will enter this

Team USA is all smiles. They are ready to do their thing...and their thing is winning.

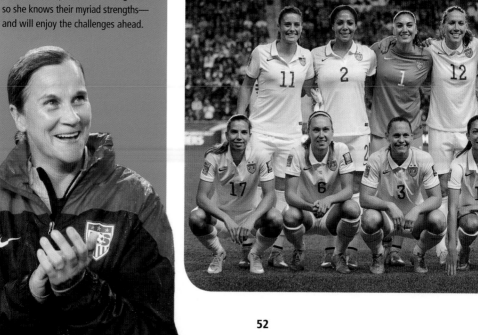

KEY PLAYER

ALEX MORGAN
Born: July 2, 1989

Morgan is a hard-working, highly competitive, and speedy striker with a clinical eye for goal, who really proved her world-class credentials in 2012 when she netted 14 goals in 12 internationals. At the age of 17 she suffered a cruciate ligament injury, but returned to score the tournament-winning goal at the FIFA U-20 Women's World Cup 2008 in Chile. She went on to win the Women's Professional Soccer championship with Western New York Flash in 2011 and Olympic gold with the USA in 2012. She was the youngest player on the roster in the FIFA Women's World Cup 2011 and scored in the final against Japan, but had to settle for a runner-up medal. She suffered an ankle injury in the Canada 2015 qualifying campaign, but when fit she is the established spearhead of arguably the world's most dangerous offensive line.

WORLD CUP RECORD

Year	Venue	Result
1991	China	Winners
1995	Sweden	Third place
1999	USA	Winners
2003	USA	Third place
2007	China	Third place
2011	Germany	Runner-up

A Women's World Cup with painful memories of having lost in the final four years ago.

That year Japan's Nadeshiko broke USA hearts when it held its collective nerve to win the penalty shoot-out that denied the Americans a first FIFA Women's World Cup title since 1999.

English-born Ellis will lead the USA team into the tournament this time around, and she knows that her job is to bring the trophy home. She will tackle the task positively—she has already stated a desire to build on the style of her predecessor Pia Sundhage—and her deployment of an attacking 4–3–3 formation in the CONCACAF Women's Championship bodes well for Canada 2015.

Captain Rampone is the only USA player to possess a FIFA Women's World Cup–winner's medal; as it embarks on a seventh consecutive appearance in the tournament, this current crop knows that nothing but an outright victory will do.

LOOK OUT FOR

CHRISTIE RAMPONE
Born: June 24, 1975
Position: Defender

An inspirational and reliable captain, this mother of two became in 2014 the second player ever to make 300 international appearances, the first one being world-record cap holder and USA legend Kristine Lilly. Rampone made her national team debut in 1997; part of the USA's FIFA Women's World Cup 1999 winning squad, she went on to collect three Olympic gold medals. She steered Sky Blue FC to the Women's Professional Soccer championship as a coach in 2009.

LAUREN HOLIDAY
Born: September 30, 1987
Position: Midfielder

Holiday is a classy player, conducting the team from midfield with her visionary passes. She played with boys' teams until the age of 12 and later was part of the USA's FIFA U-20 Women's World Championship 2006 squad, which came in fourth; her senior debut was in 2007. Her impact was felt at the FIFA Women's World Cup 2011; with two goals and a place in the all-star squad, she won praise for her clinical finishing, passing, and dead-ball ability. She changed her surname from Cheney after marrying NBA favorite Jrue Holiday in 2013.

MEGAN RAPINOE
Born: July 5, 1985
Position: Midfielder/Forward

Rapinoe scored directly from a corner kick at the London 2012 Olympics semifinal and has the ability to light up a game. She played on the USA team that finished third in the FIFA U-19 Women's World Championship in 2004. She tore her cruciate ligament in 2006 and 2007, but made it back to be a key player as the USA finished runner-up in the senior edition in 2011. She gained European soccer experience at Olympique Lyonnais in France in 2013 while on loan from her parent club, Seattle Reign FC.

AUSTRALIA

MATILDAS READY TO PRESS FOR SUCCESS

Expectations are high as Australia make its sixth finals appearance at the FIFA Women's World Cup. The Matildas have reached the quarters on the last two editions. Can they raise their game further this time?

COACH

ALEN STAJCIC

Stajcic stepped in as interim coach to guide Australia through its crucial FIFA Women's World Cup qualifying competition after the departure of former boss Hesterine de Reus. He hit the ground running to earn a qualification in Canada and took over as permanent head coach in September 2014. He played for teams in the New South Wales Premier League and attained his coaching badges in his 20s, going on to lead successful W-League side Sydney FC. The 41-year-old is well-respected in the women's game Down Under, having coached at the NSW Institute of Sport and with Sydney FC, and believes in positive, attack-minded soccer—a style to excite any World Cup fan.

There is no reason why not, given the dynamic crop of players who ensured that the Matildas qualified for 2015 with relatively little fuss.

Australia needed to finish in the top five at the AFC Women's Asian Cup in Vietnam in May 2014 to book a qualification at this year's FIFA tournament. The team arrived in Ho Chi Minh City in a state of managerial flux, with an interim head coach in Alen Stajcic—but it answered his call for positive, possession soccer to finish as group runner-up and qualify for Canada.

Of course, there was even more at stake for the Matildas in Vietnam; Australia's women became part of the Asian confederation in 2006 and made history when they won the AFC Women's Asian

Cup in 2010. They were eager to retain their title, and a 2–1 semifinal win over ever-improving Korea Republic gave them the springboard to do so—but then they needed to overcome FIFA Women's World Cup holders Japan in the final.

Having already drawn 2–2 with the Nadeshiko in the group stages—a game Australia let slip after storming into a two-goal lead—the Matildas went into the showpiece match determined to play a pressing game.

Blessed with youth and experience, an attack-minded Matildas team pushed Japan

Will the talented Matildas come of age and waltz out of their "group of death"?

KEY PLAYER

KATE GILL
Born: December 10, 1984

This prolific striker only made her debut for the Matildas in 2004 (against the nation of her birth, New Zealand, in the Australia Cup). Yet by 2014 Gill had already beaten the legendary Cheryl Salisbury's 38-goal strike record to become the nation's leading scorer. Tall and skillful, she is a veteran of the FIFA Women's World Cup 2007 but missed out on the 2011 edition through injury—so she will be eager to show her prowess in 2015. She won the AFC Women's Asian Cup with Australia in 2010 and was named best female player in Asia, then joined Perth Glory FC in 2009 and went on to top-score her way to the W-League Golden Boot gong in 2013. In recent years she's gained valuable experience by playing stints in Sweden's high-octane Damallsvenskan.

WORLD CUP RECORD

Year	Venue	Result
1991	China	Did not qualify
1995	Sweden	Group stage (4th, Group C)
1999	USA	Group stage (3rd, Group D)
2003	USA	Group stage (4th, Group D)
2007	China	Quarterfinalists
2011	Germany	Quarterfinalists

the way, but the title was lost thanks to single goal from Azusa Iwashimizu. Looking ahead, however, there is still cause for optimism for the team from Down Under as it faces an even keener test Canada.

Since showing their elite potential with first-ever win in the FIFA Women's World Cup at the 2007 edition, the women in green and gold have twice reached the last eight.

In 2011 they did so having had to bed-in up-and-coming youngsters following the retirements of key players in the run-up to the competition. The bulk of that 2011 squad continues to feature for a national team that is now even more experienced, thanks to Australia's increasingly competitive W-League.

Leading Australia into this exciting next stage, the now-permanent Stajcic hopes his group can further develop its consistency, maturity, and tactical instincts.

Given past achievements, his charges will surely work their socks off to make that happen.

LOOK OUT FOR

CAITLIN FOORD
Born: November 11, 1994
Position: Defender/Midfielder

Only 16 when she ran out for Australia in the FIFA Women's World Cup 2011, Foord made such an impact in Germany as an overlapping fullback that she went on to be named best young player of the tournament. This versatile 20-year-old is classed as one of Australia's most exciting players ever. She has W-League experience with Sydney FC and Perth Glory, and has played for Sky Blue in the US National Women's Soccer League.

CLARE POLKINGHORNE
Born: February 1, 1989
Position: Defender

The 2010 Australian female player of the year and W-League player of the year in 2013 is a veteran of the Matildas' last two FIFA Women's World Cups. A confident and capable leader and dangerous at set pieces, she has captained W-League side Brisbane Roar and cocaptains the Matildas with Kate Gill. Polkinghorne also was part of the 2010 AFC Women's Asian Cup winning team. She gained experience in the Japanese Nadeshiko League in 2014, playing for INAC Kobe Leonessa.

LISA DE VANNA
Born: November 14, 1984
Position: Forward

A star for the Matildas in the FIFA Women's World Cup 2007 after bagging four goals, De Vanna still has that wow factor going into 2015. She was crowned Australia player of the year in 2013 when a wonder goal saw her shortlisted for the FIFA Puskas Award. A lively character, capable of unlocking any defense with her determination and explosive burst of pace, she is one of the Matildas' leading scorers and has played in Australia, Europe, and America.

SWEDEN

THE SWEDES SET THEIR SIGHTS ON SILVERWARE

Sweden finished second and third in previous editions of the FIFA Women's World Cu[...] After qualifying for 2015, the Blagult have set their sights on becoming medal winne[...] once again.

COACH

PIA SUNDHAGE
One of the game's most successful figures, as a player Sundage won numerous Swedish league and cup titles. Capped 146 times—the first coming when she was 15—she scored 71 goals and won European gold in 1984 and bronze in the FIFA Women's World Cup 1991. She coached Sweden's youth teams and became assistant at Philadelphia Charge in the US Women's United Soccer Association in 2001. Sundhage went on to coach the Boston Breakers to the regular season title and was assistant to China PR coach Marika Domanski Lyfors in the FIFA Women's World Cup 2007. In five years as USA's head coach, she won FIFA Women's World Cup silver and two Olympic golds. She joined Sweden in 2012. A music lover, she was given a guitar as a parting gift by the USA players and has been known to light up press conferences by bursting into song.

Tough and technical, the Swedes were definitely in winning form in qualification, and they went into their final group match in September 2014 unbeaten. Their opponents in the deciding qualifier, however, was second-placed Scotland, and there was little margin for error—the Blagult needed to avoid a 3–1 loss or worse to steer clear of the playoffs. Pia Sundhage's team duly delivered a 2–0 win, Therese Sjogran and Lotta Schelin both scoring against the Scots in front of a rapturous crowd and their "Camp Sweden" fans in Gothenburg.

That Sjogran and Schelin's goals had booked Sweden's place in the 2015 finals was fitting: the former was making her 199th appearance, while the latter had equaled the scoring record of 72 set by the legendary Hanna Ljungberg. Not that th[...] achievements were uppermost in their minds: "Priority number one was securir[...] the World Cup spot," said Schelin. "A m[...] is absolutely what we are going for now[...]

Going for it is something Sweden has done consistently since Sundhage's pen[...] kick secured the first-ever European women's title in 1984. Runner-up spots [...] the 1987, 1995, and 2001 UEFA Women[...] Euros and the FIFA Women's World Cup 2003 all followed.

Yet gold continues to elude the Swede[...] in the modern era, and in 2013 they wer[...]

This Swedish team may be in a tough gro[...] but when it comes to the big tournamen[...] they are always contenders.

KEY PLAYER

LOTTA SCHELIN
Born: February 27, 1984

Tall, fast, and stylish, she is a clever and unselfish team player—and Sweden's all-time top striker, too. Schelin outscored her teammates in qualification, with 12 goals in 10 appearances. She won the Golden Boot in the UEFA Women's Euro 2013 and was named to the all-star squad. Since making her debut against France in 2004, the 31-year-old has gone on to play in eight major international tournaments and was on the all-star team of the FIFA Women's World Cup 2011. She has won the UEFA Women's Champions League and numerous league titles with Olympique Lyonnais. A multiple winner of the Swedish Football Association's Diamond Ball for the nation's foremost player, she was crowned best female player in the country in 2013 by the French players' union.

WORLD CUP RECORD

Year	Venue	Result
1991	China	Third place
1995	Sweden	Quarterfinalists
1999	USA	Quarterfinalists
2003	USA	Runner-up
2007	China	Group stage (3rd, Group B)
2011	Germany	Third place

...ly disappointed to lose to Germany ...he UEFA Women's Euro semifinals ...ome soil. Afterward Sundhage said ...eden would have to go from "good ...etter" if it was to clinch that elusive ...A Women's World Cup crown in 2015 in ...ada.

Going into the qualifiers, the coach kept faith with the majority of her Euro squad, and she was rewarded with a string of solid wins during which they conceded just one goal. Those victories were punctuated by a mixed bag of results that included a 1–0 win over the USA in the Algarve Cup but a 2–1 loss to Iceland in the playoff for third place, and then a 4–0 friendly loss to England in August 2014.

But when Sweden faced Scotland in the crucial qualifying match for Canada, Sundhage felt her insistence on possession soccer concentrated in the middle of the park had finally clicked. She declared: "The players have accepted the system, and we'll only keep improving from here."

LOOK OUT FOR

...ILLA FISCHER
...orn: August 2, 1984
...osition: Defender

...witched from midfield to central ...efense by Sundhage, Fischer has ...aken to the role so well she was ...amed defender of the year in 2013 by ...he Swedish FA. Great in the air and ...ith fine technical ability, she is ...nother 30-something with well over ...00 caps for her country. She made the ...ll-star squad of the UEFA Women's ...uro 2013 and just missed out on the ...014 UEFA European Player of the Year ...ong. She has won the UEFA Women's ...hampions League with VfL Wolfsburg.

ELIN RUBENSSON
Born: May 11, 1993
Position: Defender

Rubensson shone in the 2012 UEFA European Women's Under-19 Championship, top-scoring to guide Sweden to victory and earning a reputation as a big game player in the process. Named breakthrough player of 2012 by the Swedish FA, she made her debut for Sweden's seniors in late 2012. Versatile and dependable, she has played at left-back, midfield, and in attack. She is a four-time Damallsvenskan title winner with LdB FC Malmo, now known as FC Rosengard.

CAROLINE SEGER
Born: March 19, 1985
Position: Midfielder

A hardworking leader, Seger is so influential that Sundhage changed the Swedish system to "get the most" out of her. She certainly played her part in qualifying, scoring five in nine matches. She joined Paris Saint-Germain in 2014 and has played in the US Women's Professional Soccer league, captaining Western New York Flash to the title in 2011. A veteran of many elite international tournaments, she shares the Sweden captaincy with Schelin.

NIGERIA

AFRICAN CHAMPIONS ARE NOT TO BE UNDERESTIMATED

Nigeria has qualified for every edition of the FIFA Women's World Cup finals. No elite opponent would dare dream of taking the Super Falcons lightly, but how high can th nation fly in 2015?

COACH

EDWIN OKON

Okon coached the Falconets to a creditable fourth-place finish in the FIFA U-20 Women's World Cup in 2012 and was asked to take over as caretaker of the senior team in 2013 after having been an assistant previously. He oversaw the return of the African Women's Championship title to Nigeria in 2014 and, with it, qualification for the nation's seventh successive FIFA Women's World Cup, maintaining its status as the only African team to have featured in every edition. A successful coach of Nigerian club Rivers Angels, he believes in teamwork and is unafraid to mix experience and youth in the quest for success.

The last time Nigeria really shone on the main world stage was in 1999, when it put on a stunning display in a quarterfinal encounter with Brazil, coming back from 3–0 down only to lose 4–3 to Sissi's golden goal in extra time.

That finish remains Nigeria's best at any senior FIFA Women's World Cup, but in every edition that has followed, it has declared a determination to better that record.

The team has not gone beyond the group stages since. In 2011 it was stymied by a difficult draw that pitted it against giants of the game Germany and France. It headed home with its pride intact after losing by a single goal to both those opponents while beating Canada 1–0, with a squad that featured a host of players with experien of FIFA U-17 and U-20 Women's World Cups.

Under new boss Edwin Okon, that emphasis on youth continues, and the squad has been rebuilt since faring poo in the African Women's Championship i 2012. In October 2014, when it regaine title, it did so with a physically strong a athletic 21-woman squad that ranged i age from 17 to 38.

Stars such as Sweden-based Perpetua Nkwocha, four-time FIFA Women's Worl Cup veteran Stella Mbachu, and goalke

Strong and ***athletic*** are always words us to describe Nigeria; with this lineup, you add ***exciting*** to the list.

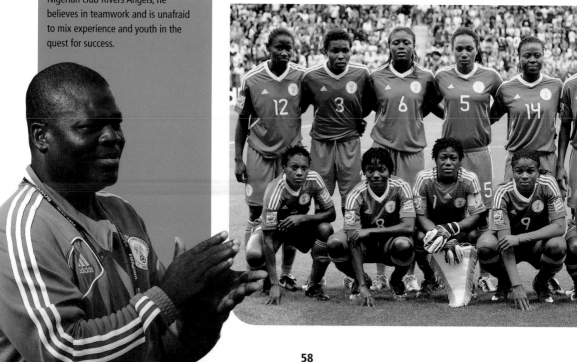

KEY PLAYER

ASISAT OSHOALA
Born: October 9, 1994

The Super Falcons may well have found a successor to their star player Perpetua Nkwocha in this talented and versatile youngster. Capable of spectacular goals, she stood out in the FIFA U-20 Women's World Cup 2014 in Canada, where she won the Golden Boot and Ball after scoring seven goals and winning three Player of the Match awards. She was awarded a national honor by Nigerian president Goodluck Jonathan after the tournament. Only age 20 when Nigeria lifted its seventh African Women's Championship title in October 2014, she was named the most valuable player of the tournament. Thought to be on the wish list of several European clubs, she rounded off the year winning both African Women's Player of the Year and Youth Player of the Year.

WORLD CUP RECORD

Year	Venue	Result
1991	China	Group stage (4th, Group C)
1995	Sweden	Group stage (4th, Group B)
1999	USA	Quarterfinalists
2003	USA	Group stage (4th, Group A)
2007	China	Group stage (4th, Group B)
2011	Germany	Group stage (3rd, Group A)

...cious Dede returned to bring their vast ...erience to the team.

...ut 11 of the players who clinched the ...d-fought 2–0 victory over Cameroon, ...ich secured a record seventh African ...men's Championship title for Nigeria, ...e age 23 and under.

...kon insists there are no stars in this Nigeria squad, and his teams were solid from front to back throughout the tournament in Namibia. But two of his promising youngsters eclipsed the opposition to receive honors at the tournament's close, with France-based forward Desire Oparanozie top-scoring, while FIFA U-20 Women's World Cup 2014 starlet Asisat Oshoala was named most valuable player.

Such a wealth of young talent suggests that Nigeria will continue to be a nation to watch when the FIFA Women's World Cup kicks off.

And if the team receives the support enjoyed by other elite sides, Nigeria will go from strength to strength.

LOOK OUT FOR

NGOZI EBERE
Born: August 5, 1991
Position: Defender

A hardworking and forceful left-back who likes to get forward and take responsibility for set pieces, Ebere has progressed from the under-20s to the senior setup and put on a player-of-the-match performance in the 2014 African Women's Championship, setting up two goals and impressing technical experts with her work rate. A key defender for Nigeria in the qualification tournament, this determined player will be difficult to beat in Canada.

EVELYN NWABUOKU
Born: November 14, 1985
Position: Defender/Midfielder

The Super Falcons' versatile captain is a reassuring presence on the pitch, where she leads by example with her coolness under pressure, quick feet, and incisive passing. She experienced the FIFA U-19 Women's World Championship 2004 and has gone on to become an integral member of the senior side, more than playing her part in the Super Falcons' qualification for Canada 2015. Nwabuoku has led Nigerian Women's Premier League team Rivers Angels to domestic honors.

DESIRE OPARANOZIE
Born: December 17, 1993
Position: Forward

Tenacious and powerful, Oparanozie made her mark in the FIFA U-17 and U-20 Women's World Cups and was a key figure for the under-20 Falconets in 2010, when Nigeria went all the way to a final matchup against eventual winners Germany; she was ever-present when they finished fourth in 2012. She started all three games in the senior 2011 edition, including the 1–0 win over Canada, and has European experience with FC Rossiyanka of Russia and Guingamp in France.

The Olympic Stadium in Montreal is the largest venue at the FIFA Women's World Cup 2015.

GROUP E

ith ever-present finals contender Brazil playing
more competitive Korea Republic team than
e one they dismissed in 2003—with three goals
ithout reply—and the intriguing prospect of
ain taking on fellow debut team Costa Rica,
cording a solid opening result could be key to
is finely poised group.

BRAZIL

CAN THE YELLOW JERSEYS OF BRAZIL LIGHT UP CANADA 2015?

Brazil is the only team from South America to have reached every edition of the FIFA Women's World Cup. The naturally talented As Canarinhas players came within a whisper of gold in 2007. How will this group fare in 2015?

COACH

OSWALDO ALVAREZ
Known as Vadao, the experienced 58-year-old is renowned for his work in men's soccer, having coached in Brazil's Serie A, B, and C at clubs including Corinthians and São Paulo. He boasts a reputation as a student of the game and is also known for his ability to bring through young players—he is said to have discovered world-class stars such as Rivaldo and Kaka. Tactically and defensively astute while also being attack-minded, he took over the women's national team in 2014 and has described it as one of his biggest challenges yet. He negotiated the first hurdle by ensuring that Brazil reached Canada 2015.

Certainly Brazil shone brightly enough in the Copa America Femenina competition that decided which two of 10 South American teams would directly make it to the 2015 edition. Despite heading to Ecuador in September 2014 without star striker Marta in the squad, Oswaldo Alvarez's players bossed the championship, losing just one match of seven in 17 intense days of soccer.

Veteran forward Cristiane, 37-year-old keeper Andreia, and exciting youngsters such as defender Tayla stepped up to the plate as the challenges of Bolivia, Paraguay, Chile, and Ecuador were all comfortably dismissed.

A 2–0 defeat by Argentina in the group phase was the only downside of the tournament, although that largely reserve team loss was avenged with a comprehensive 6–0 victory over Las Albicelestes in the final phase.

Colombia proved a more stubborn opponent in the last match, but the resulting 0–0 draw between the two was enough for both nations to qualify for Canada 2015. "It's been a brilliant campaign," said Vadao afterward.

Indeed it was, given that Brazil had not only qualified for the FIFA Women's World Cup—it had claimed a sixth South American Championship title, too. Such

Brazil is always full of flair, and with Rio 2 on the horizon, this team might be more prepared than any of its predecessors.

MARTA
Born: February 19, 1986

What can be said about the five-time FIFA Women's World Player of the Year? One of the world's best-known female players, she possesses unparalleled speed on the ball. She first lit up the world stage in the FIFA U-19 Women's World Championship 2002, winning the Silver Ball before going on to claim the Golden Ball in the 2004 edition. She won Olympic silver that year, too—but she really came to the fore in the FIFA Women's World Cup 2007 in China, when she scored seven goals and ran off with the Golden Shoe and Golden Ball gongs. Currently sharing the top all-time FIFA Women's World Cup goalscorer record with Birgit Prinz, she has won multiple titles with clubs in Sweden and America.

WORLD CUP RECORD

Year	Venue	Result
1991	China	Group stage (3rd, Group B)
1995	Sweden	Group stage (4th, Group A)
1999	USA	Third place
2003	USA	Quarterfinalists
2007	China	Runner-up
2011	Germany	Quarterfinalists

...ination of its own confederation has ...to be repeated on the world stage, ...ever.

...nce Brazil's breakthrough in 1999, it ...always reached the quarterfinals of the ...Women's World Cup, but it has yet to ...er 2007's showing of second.

...nd while the team's Olympic record ...en more impressive, with two silver medals and two fourth-place finishes achieved, its failure to progress beyond the quarterfinals at the London 2012 Olympics was disappointing, to say the least.

Since then, though, more regular participation in friendlies as well as its own annual invitational tournament ought to have given its gifted individuals the opportunity to develop together as a smart unit and gel as a formidable squad.

Striving for that cohesion is particularly vital when so many players have gone abroad in search of improved playing opportunities. Given the ever-shrinking margins for error at the elite level, tactical understanding and the ability to react and adapt to changing situations is key. For As Canarinhas this summer, that might just be the difference between promising and delivering.

LOOK OUT FOR

ORMIGA
orn: March 3, 1978
osition: Midfielder

...ball-winning defensive midfielder of ...e highest order, this 37-year-old has ...arned the respect of her peers at the ...ite level and is a symbol of the ...omen's game in Brazil. Formiga has ...epresented her country in every FIFA ...omen's World Cup since 1995 and is ...e only player to have appeared at ...ery Olympics since 1996. She has ...rned out for several clubs in Brazil as ...ell as Malmo FF in Sweden and New ...rsey Wildcats, FC Gold Pride, and ...hicago Red Stars in America.

CRISTIANE
Born: May 15, 1985
Position: Forward

This punchy, intelligent, and powerful striker came through the youth ranks alongside Marta, with whom she has enjoyed a deadly partnership over the years. She scored the fastest hat trick in the women's Olympics in 2008 and was the competition's top scorer. She has twice come third in the FIFA Women's World Player of the Year awards, and experts described her as "exceptional" in the FIFA Women's World Cup 2007. She has loads of experience, having played in Brazil, Europe, and America.

ANDRESSA
Born: May 1, 1995
Position: Forward

A gifted player, also known as Andressinha, Andressa is seen by many in Brazil as the closest to Marta when it comes to natural talent. She plays with flair as well as passion and excelled at youth level in the creative number 10 role. She has been labeled "captain extraordinaire" for her performances in youth championships in South America and has also appeared for Brazil in FIFA U-17 and U-20 Women's World Cups, earning praise for her ability to read the game.

KOREA REPUBLIC
TALENTED TAEGUK LADIES AIM HIGH

Korea Republic could well be one of the dark horses of the FIFA Women's World Cup 2015. The team debuted in the 2003 tournament, but has not won a game and or qualified since—until now. A challenge awaits. Can Korea Republic rise to it?

COACH

YOON DEOK-YEO

Having represented his country as a player, this coach knows how it feels to play on the biggest stage of all. The 54-year-old former defender, who expects his teams to defend well, too, played for Korea Republic during its first-round exit at the 1990 FIFA World Cup. The experience he garnered as a player in the domestic K-League has not been lost—he turned to coaching. Several K-League clubs and the Korea Republic boys' team that played in the FIFA U-17 World Championship in 2003 have all benefited from his expertise. Joining the women's team in 2013, he oversaw a high-scoring qualification campaign.

If gifted playmaker Ji So-yun is a yardstick for the level of talent available to coach Yoon Deok-yeo, then the team should fare well. Blessed with superb vision and even better ball control, Ji lit up the FA Women's Super League in England in 2014, and she is desperate for her team to do the same in Canada this summer.

"Of course our aim is to win," she said. "I believe if you are a football player, you must always aim high and play to win the World Cup."

The Taeguk Ladies disappointed in the 2003 edition, but the Korea Republic we can expect to see in 2015 is well-equipped for tournament play. A host of players have gained experience at FIFA underage championships, and they are quick and tidy players, boasting great technique and a hard edge.

Ji's strike partner Yeo Min-ji and dyna midfielder Lee So-dam were FIFA U-17 Women's World Cup winners in 2010 ar along with several of that year's bronze winning FIFA U-20 Women's World Cup side, are now part of the senior setup.

Complementing these rising stars of Asian soccer are veterans such as Park Eun-sun, who top-scored as Korea Repu qualified for the FIFA Women's World C 2015 via the AFC Women's Asian Cup.

Coach Yoon Deok-yeo's squad needed

Many of the Taeguk Ladies, pictured her the 2014 Asian Games, have won medals the youth level.

JI SO-YUN
Born: February 21, 1991

Anyone who witnessed four-time Korean Player of the Year play for Chelsea Ladies in the English FA Women's Super League in 2014 will know that she is something special. Small and compact, Ji has the ability to baffle defenders with her dribbling skills, but she is no showboater—she can score and bring other players into the game, too. Ideally she likes to play in the number 10 role, but as her displays for Chelsea have proved, she is flexible and willing to play anywhere across the forward line or in midfield. Ji made her debut for Korea at the tender age of 15 and went on to play in Japan for INAC Kobe Leonessa. She signed a two-year deal with Chelsea in January 2014 and was named FA WSL Players' Player of the Year in her first season.

WORLD CUP RECORD

Year	Venue	Result
1991	China	Did not qualify
1995	Sweden	Did not qualify
1999	USA	Did not qualify
2003	USA	Group stage (4th, Group B)
2007	China	Did not qualify
2011	Germany	Did not qualify

e one of the top five teams in the petition in Vietnam in May 2014 to k a spot in Canada, and Park bossed the ing charts as the Koreans obliterated nmar 12–0 and beat fellow 2015 ifiers Thailand 4–0.

ose results were enough to see them through to Canada, and they concluded their group with a goalless draw against China PR.

Park's second-half penalty kept her team in the semifinal against Australia that followed, but the Koreans were overcome 2–1 in Ho Chi Minh City.

If that was a bitter pill, the loss to China by a late-late goal in the battle for third place in Thong Nhat Stadium was even harder to swallow.

Yet while Yoon felt the team's physicality was lacking against the Matildas, he was pleased with his charges and expects them to push on when they reach the ultimate world stage.

OOK OUT FOR

EE SO-DAM
orn: October 12, 1994
osition: Midfielder

ready a veteran of three underage FA Women's World Cups, this lively idfielder is energetic and confident. essed with great balance—she is a atural at tae kwon do, too—she also as great positional awareness. She ves to supply pinpoint crosses and ee kicks and puts in the hours on the aining pitch to get them inch-perfect. nall in stature, she's a big game ayer nonetheless, scoring in the final help her country lift the FIFA U-17 omen's World Cup in 2010.

PARK EUN-SUN
Born: December 25, 1986
Position: Forward

It is 12 years since striker Park first lit up the international scene. Tall and strong, she played every one of Korea's FIFA Women's World Cup 2003 games and she was only 16. She has since said the competition came too soon for her—but she is ready for 2015. Park left Korea for Russian team FC Rossiyanka and, despite a long hiatus from international soccer, she can still produce at the elite level, as her goals in the 2014 AFC Women's Asian Cup showed.

YEO MIN-JI
Born: April 27, 1993
Position: Forward

Yeo enjoyed a breakthrough international season in 2010, winning the FIFA U-17 Women's World Cup, the tournament's Golden Ball and Boot, and the AFC Women's Youth Player of the Year gong. A determined goal-getter, she can have fans up on their feet in appreciation of her maze-like runs. And run she can, with a great engine, plus balance and poise. Yeo has developed a great understanding with Ji So-yun and is definitely one to watch.

SPAIN
LA ROJA LOOK TO BUILD ON HISTORIC DEBUT

Spain has never qualified for the FIFA Women's World Cup before now, but with a rising reputation, it was only a matter of time before it did. So how far will these newcomers go?

COACH

IGNACIO QUEREDA

"Nacho" has led the women's team since 1988. The 64-year-old played on the wing for Real Madrid's youth team and coached men's team CD Mostoles in Spain's third division before teaming up with the women's national squad. In 2004 he led Spain's UEFA European Women's Under-19 Championship–winning team, and he took the seniors to an impressive quarterfinal qualification at the UEFA Women's Euro 2013, the nation's first major finals in 16 years. A respected technician of the game, he has brought through several youth players into the senior setup and enjoyed the fruits of his labor when Spain qualified for the FIFA Women's World Cup 2015, its third major senior tournament under his charge.

La Roja was as successful as it was possible to be when it came to qualification for Canada, winning Group 2 with a game to go thanks to Natalia Pablos's brace in a 2–0 victory away to Romania. Estonia, FYR Macedonia, Czech Republic, and tricky Italy were also dismissed on the road to Canada 2015 as Spain finished three points clear of the Azzurre, the only team to take points off them in an unbeaten campaign.

Spain's historic achievement was well met by a soccer-obsessed nation, and they made headlines across the country. There were bravos aplenty on social media, too, with Spain and Manchester United goalkeeper David de Gea sending "las chicas" his congratulations via Twitter. The plaudits were merited, given the flair with

which Spain had qualified, and its Europ rivals quickly discovered that what La R lacks in size, it more than makes up for work rate and talent.

The squad that secured qualification featured the core of the team that had s impressed when Spain reached the last eight of the UEFA Women's Euro 2013. In the aftermath of that tournament in Sweden, Spain was noted as technically gifted by official observers, who also compared them favorably to the men's national side that had recently won a h trick of major titles.

La Roja feel like they've been so close fo so many years; now they are Canada-bo and raring to go.

VERONICA BOQUETE

Born: April 9, 1987

With outstanding technical ability, two good feet, and playmaking vision, Spain's cocaptain will delight FIFA Women's World Cup audiences. Hardworking and hungry, she believes in herself and her team. She won the 2004 UEFA European Women's Under-19 Championship and was named to the all-star team of the FIFA U-19 Women's World Championship that same year. In 2005 she took her senior bow and made the all-star squad of the UEFA Women's Euro 2013. Boquete picks up plaudits wherever she plays, most impressively in the US, where she was named Michelle Akers Women's Professional Soccer League Player of the Year in 2011 and Portland Thorns FC supporters' Player of 2014. In Sweden she was crowned Midfielder of the Year after winning the league with Tyreso FF in 2012. She played soccer with German outfit 1. FFC Frankfurt in 2014.

WORLD CUP RECORD

Conceding only two goals in its whole qualifying campaign, Spain is on its way to its first ever FIFA Women's World Cup.

igh praise indeed—and Spain's
k attacks and short, sharp passing
me successfully propelled the team
the quarterfinals of the competition,
hough eventual silver medal winners

Norway won out 3–1.

Long-standing coach Ignacio Quereda maintained that Spain still needed to build its "big-match experience" when it left Scandinavia. Several of his players

already have that, a handful having won gold either in the 2004 UEFA European Women's Under-19 Championship or the Under-17 Championship in 2010 and 2011. Domestically, the squad is gaining experience, too. Several players competed in highly competitive leagues in Europe and America in 2014, while others tasted UEFA Women's Champions League soccer with FC Barcelona.

The FIFA Women's World Cup will be Spain's biggest test to date, but with the wealth of talent at its disposal, it will work hard to make it a debut to remember.

LOOK OUT FOR

MARTA TORREJON

Born: February 27, 1990
Position: Defender

Torrejon played soccer with boys until age 14 and is a solid central defender who leads by example. She captained Spain in the UEFA European Women's Under-19 Championship in 2007 and 2008 as well as RCD Espanyol, where he won league and cup honors. Her awards continued after joining Barcelona. In 2007 she debuted for Spain's seniors and was featured in every game of the UEFA Women's Euro 2013 and all 10 qualifiers for Canada. Her brother Marc is a professional player.

JENNIFER HERMOSO

Born: May 9, 1990
Position: Midfielder/Forward

Hermoso is a versatile attacker with a great left foot who loves to set up goals as well as score them. She made the goal that won Rayo Vallecano the Spanish title in 2011 and gained experience in the demanding Swedish Damallsvenskan with Tyreso before joining Barcelona in 2014. She made her senior debut for Spain in 2012 and was ever-present as La Roja made the quarterfinals of the UEFA Women's Euro 2013, scoring twice. She bagged seven goals in 10 qualifiers.

NATALIA PABLOS

Born: October 15, 1985
Position: Forward

An instinctive finisher who won multiple titles with Rayo Vallecano, Pablos captained the club and scored over 300 goals in nearly 13 years. She left in 2013 to join Bristol Academy WFC in the English FA Women's Super League, then under current England coach Mark Sampson, and moved to Arsenal for the 2015 season. Another of Spain's 2004 UEFA European Women's Under-19 Championship victors, she scored 12 goals in 10 qualifying games.

COSTA RICA

LAS TICAS TAKING THEIR RAPID RISE IN STRIDE

Costa Rica became the first Central American team to qualify for Canada 2015. Its achievement shows how far the women's game has advanced in this small but ambitious soccer-playing nation—but it knows this is still a work in progress.

COACH

AMELIA VALVERDE

When then head coach Carlos Garabet Avedissian announced his departure in January 2015, one of his assistants, 28-year-old Amelia Valverde was appointed as his replacement. A central defender with first-division team Flores for eight years, Valverde then served as its head coach for a further two. In 2011 she joined Costa Rica as conditioning coach, progressing to assistant with the under-20s and seniors, and then head of the under-17s. She knows the players and system well, and she will relish the responsibility of taking her team to the world stage.

A third-place finish in 1998 was Costa Rica's previous best at a CONCACAF Women's World Cup qualifying tournament, but in 2014 the team managed to finish as runner-up, losing only to the USA in the final and playing an entertaining brand of soccer in the process.

Along the way, Las Ticas beat Mexico for the first time ever, and they bossed Trinidad and Tobago in the semifinal, although it eventually took a penalty shoot-out to settle that match in their favor and guarantee an automatic qualification for the FIFA Women's World Cup 2015.

"There's nothing to do but celebrate," said Costa Rica goalkeeper Dinnia Diaz after performing heroics during the shoot-out and saving three spot kicks. "You celebrate

because we're in the World Cup. In the er it's not just the team, but the country tha celebrates this victory."

Given that Costa Ricans came out in record numbers to watch the FIFA U-17 Women's World Cup in March 2014, it do indeed look as though the nation is behin the women's game. Costa Rican presiden Luis Guillermo Solis reflected the mood o the country when he telephoned then hea coach Carlos Garabet Avedissian to congratulate him on achieving qualificatio for Canada 2015.

A humbling 6–0 loss to the USA in the

Las Ticas may be outsized by some of their opponents, but they will not be outfought.

EY PLAYER

SHIRLEY CRUZ
Born: August 28, 1985

Cruz has blazed a trail for female soccer players in Costa Rica and is ahead of the curve in terms of her ability and development, so it will be great to see her feature at a FIFA Women's World Cup while still in her prime. She moved to France to join Olympique Lyonnais in 2006 on a semiprofessional basis. Her terrier-like work rate and technical excellence earned her a two-year professional contract with the French champions in 2009, and she was part of the all-conquering team that went on to win the UEFA Women's Champions League two years in a row. She became a regular starter for Paris Saint-Germain after signing for Lyon's rivals in 2012, and was named the best female player in France by the French Football Federation in 2013.

WORLD CUP RECORD

Costa Rica successfully hosted the FIFA U-17 Women's World Cup 2014 and is celebrating further with its first-ever qualification to the finals of the senior competition.

al that followed left Avedissian lamenting physical differences between the verful Americans and his own players: you can do really when Abby Wambach laying like this is to pray, pray that they 't get the ball to her," he joked after the ker had netted three headers in the final.

Yet what they lack in height, this Costa Rica group makes up for in unity after having played together for several years now, and after qualification their former coach was anything but downhearted about the future.

"There is really no ceiling for women's football in the country," he declared, and

not without cause. Las Ticas have played at four FIFA youth tournaments since 2008. They have yet to progress to the knockout stages of these elite competitions, but the experience of playing as a group has been invaluable in forming the core of the current senior team.

Now that they have qualified for both the FIFA Women's World Cup 2015 and the Pan American Games that follow in Canada in July, that unity and their nation's development will surely see them continue onward and upward.

OOK OUT FOR

IANA SAENZ
Born: April 15, 1989
Position: Defender

A solid, right-sided player, Saenz takes er defensive responsibilities seriously ut is always happy to attack when he opportunity arises. The fact that he was named in the CONCACAF Women's Championship 2014 Best XI s testament to her dependable, logged performances. Known for her ptimistic, positive outlook and lively ersonality, she will be a senior at the University of South Florida in 2015 nd has been almost ever-present for he Bulls in her first three years.

GLORIANA VILLALOBOS
Born: August 20, 1999
Position: Midfielder

The year 2014 was momentous for this skillful player: she was captain at the FIFA U-17 Women's World Cup on home soil in March, starred in the U-20 edition in the summer, and made her senior competitive debut, at just age 14, in the Central American Football Union (UNCAF) prequalifying tournament. A bundle of energy but also a fantastic innovator in the creative midfield role, she has drawn high praise from a range of professionals, including from Costa Rica men's coach Jorge Pinto.

KATHERINE ALVARADO
Born: April 11, 1991
Position: Midfielder

The team's cocaptain, Alvarado moved away from her village and family in the Gautuzu Valley to the capital San Jose to play soccer at age 13. She says the sacrifice was worth it to achieve her dreams of playing for her country, which she has done at a string of international tournaments, most prominently the FIFA U-17 Women's World Cup 2008 in New Zealand and the U-20 edition in Germany. She has also realized her ambition to play abroad, spending time in the Finnish league.

Moncton Stadium, with its capacity of just over 20,000, will have an exciting atmosphere when Group F kicks off there on June 9.

GROUP F

The two European teams, England and France, should be the strongest of this group. But how they both cope with Mexico and Colombia's contrasting styles and rhythm of play could dictate their destiny in a competition in which France is tipped to go far.

FRANCE
CAN LES BLEUES PLAY TO PERFECTION IN CANADA?

France qualified for its third FIFA Women's World Cup with a flawless campaign, although its manager Philippe Bergeroo insisted the team would keep its feet on the ground in the lead-up to 2015.

COACH

PHILIPPE BERGEROO

Bergeroo made his name in men's soccer, playing in goal for Bordeaux and Toulouse. He won three caps for France, was a member of the 1984 gold-medal-winning UEFA European Championship squad, and was on the roster for the 1986 FIFA World Cup in Mexico when Les Bleus finished third. He was goalkeeping coach for France's senior men's team, most notably with the 1998 FIFA World Cup–winning group, and went on to work domestically with Paris Saint-Germain and Stade Rennais. He led France's under-17 boys to UEFA Euro glory before taking over the women's side in July 2013. The 61-year-old is big on organization, quick passing, intelligent distribution, and hard work.

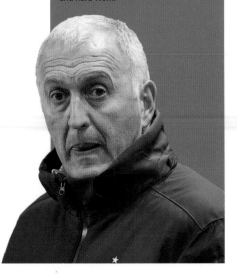

When the tournament kicks off, however, an entire nation will want it to hit the soccer turf running in the hope that it can build on its fourth-place finish in 2011 in Germany.

France recorded the same position at the Olympics in London a year later, and an athletic squad lit up the UEFA Women's Euro 2013 as well with its fast one- and two-touch technique. Les Bleues felt they were unlucky not to progress beyond the quarterfinals of that tournament, their exit coming after a penalty shoot-out loss to Denmark.

They needed to regroup afterward, not just mentally but as a unit, given that their coach Bruno Bini was replaced soon after their return by former professional

goalkeeper Bergeroo. The switch has pro a productive one; under Bergeroo, who h set the players to work on their strength in a bid to equip them for the competitiv rigors that lie in wait, they have found fr impetus.

In March 2014 the talented French stormed to a Cyprus Cup title triumph, and six months later they completed the impeccable FIFA Women's World Cup qualification campaign, scoring 54 goals while conceding three during the course 10 straight wins.

"I'm very happy," Bergeroo said once

Packed with quality, this French team is a joy to watch but a menace to play agains

KEY PLAYER

LOUISA NECIB
Born: January 23, 1987

Playmaking midfielder with a sublime touch, she is a graduate of France's youth setup, making her senior tournament debut in the UEFA Women's Euro 2005. Shortlisted for the Golden Ball in the FIFA Women's World Cup 2011, she was credited as vital to France's exciting give-and-go style in the UEFA Women's Euro 2013 in Sweden. She made the 10 best open-play goal list after she turned England's defense inside out, scored in the group stages, and was later named to the tournament's all-star squad. Necib has won the UEFA Women's Champions League with Olympique Lyonnais, as well as countless domestic titles. The 28-year-old has been described by the French media as the "female Zinedine Zidane" and by her former manager Bruno Bini as "an artist."

WORLD CUP RECORD

Year	Venue	Result
1991	China	Did not qualify
1995	Sweden	Did not qualify
1999	USA	Did not qualify
2003	USA	Group stage (3rd, Group B)
2007	China	Did not qualify
2011	Germany	Fourth place

ualification had been assured with a 2–0 victory over Finland. "The first box is ticked. We now have a full year to work. We'll stay grounded because there is a long way to .o." France certainly worked hard throughout ualification, playing friendlies with

heavyweights such as Sweden, Brazil, and the USA. The Swedes were overcome 3–0, and a goalless draw was played out against the South Americans, while France recorded a draw and a loss to USA. A strong Les Bleues team also tested itself against Germany in October 2014, and Brazil,

again, in November, emerging 2–0 victors in both games.

Results such as these will have been a boost for Bergeroo, who is benefiting from the coming of age of a host of France's former youth players from the last decade, who play their domestic soccer in France's highly rated Division 1 Feminine.

Should France take its 2014 vein of form into 2015 and Canada, Les Bleues could make their coach and their nation even happier.

LOOK OUT FOR

GRIEDGE MBOCK BATHY
Born: February 26, 1995
Position: Defender

Bathy was superb in the FIFA U-17 Women's World Cup in 2012 as Les Bleuettes won the trophy and she captured the Golden Ball. Hailed by FIFA's technical experts for her strength, reading of the game, and aerial threat, she captained France to UEFA European Women's Under-19 Championship glory in 2013. She already has experience playing in Canada—she led France to third place in the FIFA U-20 Women's World Cup in 2014.

WENDIE RENARD
Born: July 20, 1990
Position: Defender

A tall, elegant, and strong defender who has developed into a fine captain, Renard reads the game well and can play in the center or as fullback, while offering a goal threat to set pieces. She played in UEFA and FIFA tournaments with the under-19s and -20s and broke into the senior team in 2011, going on to play in that year's FIFA Women's World Cup and the 2012 Olympics. She has gained a wealth of experience in the UEFA Women's Champions League with Olympique Lyonnais.

EUGENIE LE SOMMER
Born: May 18, 1989
Position: Forward

Le Sommer brings the goals in the big games, but she can also unlock defenses and bring teammates into play with her vision and precise passing. Named to the UEFA Women's Euro 2013 all-star squad, she scored one of the top 10 best goals from open play; she also hit seven goals in eight Canada 2015 qualifiers. Crowned 2010 female player of the year by the French National Union of Professional Football Players, she won the Bronze Ball at the FIFA U-20 Women's World Cup in 2008.

ENGLAND
LIONESSES ROARING THEIR WAY TO CANADA

England surged toward qualification for the FIFA Women's World Cup with a 100 percent record. The team has reached the quarterfinals three times before—but can it beat that in 2015?

COACH

MARK SAMPSON

The 32-year-old Welshman was appointed in December 2013. He was head coach at FA Women's Super League team Bristol Academy for five years, leading them to two FA Women's Cup finals and to a WSL runner-up qualification in his final season. Sampson started to learn his coaching trade in Wales and worked under Roberto Martinez at Swansea City AFC's Centre of Excellence. Martinez is just one of the coaches he cites as a major influence on his coaching style, which seeks to create an environment that encourages creativity. He says: "We want to be brave and have courage to control our own destiny."

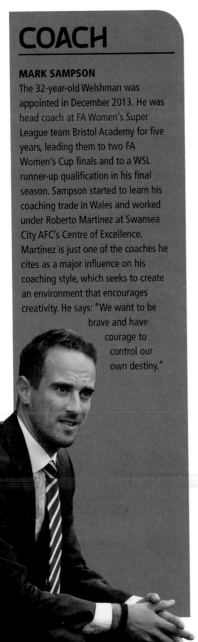

The Three Lionesses will certainly head to North America with their tails up, having booked their ticket with such aplomb— scoring a whopping 52 goals and conceding only one along the way.

Belarus, Turkey, Montenegro, Ukraine, and neighbors Wales were swept aside in qualification, with Olha Ovdiychuk's solitary goal for Ukraine the only blot on the otherwise perfect copybook of a campaign that went smoothly from first to last.

The Three Lionesses went into qualification on the back of a desperately disappointing display in Sweden at the UEFA Women's Euro 2013, where they suffered two defeats and a draw and went out in the group stage despite high expectations. The FA chose to end manager Hope Powell's era-defining 15-year reign, and up stepped assistant Brent Hills as interim manager.

With zest and confidence returning to their performances, the players put six and eight goals past Belarus and Turkey respectively without reply. By the time the FA announced Powell's permanent replacement, former Bristol Academy WFC boss Mark Sampson, in December 2013, England was four wins in, top of the group and sitting pretty.

Even so, with the change of staff came a shift in approach and a shake-up in playing personnel, too; a return to full fitness and

The Three Lionesses lineup has been refreshed under Mark Sampson and they are looking to compete with the best.

KEY PLAYER

ENIOLA ALUKO
Born: February 21, 1987

A striker capable of frighteningly fast acceleration (like her younger brother, Sone, a professional player) and very quick feet, Aluko can operate through the center, or more often down the right. Making her senior debut in 2004, she made her first big impact for England in the UEFA Women's Euro 2005. She enjoyed a notable qualifying campaign, bagging 13 goals, concluding with her first international hat trick in the 10–0 away demolition of Montenegro. Three seasons in the US Women's Professional Soccer league and then playing alongside other world greats at Chelsea has seen her mature into a dangerous weapon in Sampson's England armory. A confident Aluko is more than a handful for even the best of defenses.

WORLD CUP RECORD

Year	Venue	Result
1991	China	Did not qualify
1995	Sweden	Quarterfinalists
1999	USA	Did not qualify
2003	USA	Did not qualify
2007	China	Quarterfinalists
2011	Germany	Quarterfinalists

Sampson's faith with a goal on her full debut in a friendly against Sweden in August 2014.

In qualifying, instinctive striker Toni Duggan notched up a 10-goal tally to prove her potential to lead the line for England into the future. Meanwhile Eniola Aluko's 13 strikes served as further evidence of a player at her peak.

Sampson regularly reiterates the importance of character, mentality, and a positive attitude, and with the commitment from his players, these traits have created a potent mix.

...rm of several regulars was complemented ...a willingness to try out younger and ...urning players.

...Figures like striker Lianne Sanderson, who ...is starring for the Boston Breakers in the ...National Women's Soccer League, were ...ought back into the fold. Others, like

midfielder Jordan Nobbs and defenders Lucy Bronze and Demi Stokes, were promoted from the bench, and the under-23s became regular starters.

Francesca Kirby, playing in the second tier of English soccer at Reading, was another to be given a chance, and she rewarded

LOOK OUT FOR

STEPHANIE HOUGHTON
Born: April 23, 1988
Position: Defender

Steph Houghton became a household name after a great showing for Team GB at the London 2012 Olympic Games. She is England's new captain under Sampson, having been moved inside, from left fullback to center-back—a position she has also settled into playing for club team Manchester City WFC. A versatile all-rounder, she has determination, leadership qualities, and an eye for the goal that makes her an important part of the England team.

JORDAN NOBBS
Born: December 8,1992
Position: Midfielder

A diminutive, dynamic, box-to-box midfielder, Nobbs is a great striker of the ball, with fantastic balance and poise. At just 15 she captained England at the FIFA U-17 Women's World Cup 2008 and scored in England's victory over Sweden in the final of the 2009 UEFA European Women's Under-19 Championship. She made her senior debut in March 2013, but she really got her chance under Hills, and played her part in qualification despite suffering a back injury in early 2014.

KAREN CARNEY
Born: August 1, 1987
Position: Forward

If Kelly Smith is the most gifted female player to hail from England, then Carney must be the closest to follow in her creative footsteps. She debuted for England a decade ago and plays with passion, whether dribbling down the left flank or pulling the strings in midfield. She enjoyed spells in the US with Chicago Red Stars and in England with Arsenal, where she won plenty of silverware. Carney returned to her first club, Birmingham City, where she won the FA Women's Cup in 2012.

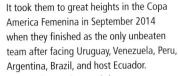

COLOMBIA

COLLECTIVE AMBITION GIVES COLOMBIA CAUSE FOR OPTIMISM

Colombia booked its second FIFA Women's World Cup qualification by being one of the top two teams in the Copa America Femenina tournament. The coach says the players are as close as a family—so how far can their cohesion carry them in Canada?

COACH

FABIAN FELIPE TABORDA

"El Profesor" became a part of Colombia's women's setup in 2012 when he took responsibility for Las Cafeteritas, as the youth teams are known. He took the under-20s to a gold medal finish in the regional multisport Bolivarian Games in 2013 and led the younger girls to the 2012 and 2014 FIFA U-17 Women's World Cups. Taborda got the senior job in 2014 and oversaw an unbeaten campaign in qualification for Canada 2015 via the Copa America Femenina. The 36-year-old also has experience at league level in Colombia as technical director of the women's section of Club Deportivo Generaciones Palmiranas, where several members of his national squad play soccer.

It took them to great heights in the Copa America Femenina in September 2014 when they finished as the only unbeaten team after facing Uruguay, Venezuela, Peru, Argentina, Brazil, and host Ecuador.

Las Cafeteras boasted the meanest defense in that competition, too, conceding twice in seven games and denying Brazil the chance to score in the final match, a goalless draw that booked both nations a spot in Canada 2015.

Their second-place finish in the final-phase group table additionally saw Colombia through to the 2015 Pan American Games, also in Canada, and the 2016 Olympics in Brazil. For now, though, the South American team is looking toward the biggest women's tournament in the

FIFA calendar and its second stab at world glory.

Colombia took a point from a tough group in the 2011 edition, drawing with Korea DPR but losing to highly rated Sweden and eventual finalists the USA. Not particularly physical on the field, the squad relied instead on skill, organization, and discipline to get it through, and although it did not make it out of its group, it left Germany that year with heads held high.

Colombia was disappointed to lose every match in the London 2012 Olympics—but its opponents did include stellar soccer-

Colombia's team is like a family of sisters, all of whom are great with a ball at their feet.

KEY PLAYER

YORELI RINCON
Born: July 27, 1993

The number 10 has been labeled Colombia's answer to Marta, and the comparison is not without justification. A vibrant and exciting player, Rincon is totally at ease with the ball at her feet. Taught to play by her brother, she has gone on to gain experience in the FIFA U-17 and U-20 Women's World Cups with her country. She made the all-star team in the 2010 U-20 edition for her skills as a playmaker. Rincon will still only be 21 when Canada 2015 kicks off—but she already has a wealth of experience, having played at club level in Brazil, Sweden, and America. She scored key goals to secure Colombia's place in both the 2011 and 2015 FIFA Women's World Cups and will be a crowd-pleaser in Canada.

WOMEN'S WORLD CUP RECORD

Year	Venue	Result
1991	China	Did not enter
1995	Sweden	Did not enter
1999	USA	Did not qualify
2003	USA	Did not qualify
2007	China	Did not qualify
2011	Germany	Group stage (4th, Group C)

...aying nations France and the USA. Las Cafeteras had some rising stars of their own in those two competitions, including several from the tight-knit group who had experienced the FIFA U-20 Women's World Cup 2010 together. Gifted strikers Lady Andrade and Ingrid ...dal, reliable defender and inspirational captain Natalia Gaitan, and attacking midfielder Tatiana Ariza are just a few to have graduated from the youth teams and become regulars for the national team.

Several new faces were bedded in during qualification too—all of which bodes well for the future of this increasingly impressive soccer nation.

"We have a close-knit team as in a family," said coach Fabian Felipe Taborda, who took over from Ricardo Rozo in 2014. "We are a team that plays good football and we are mentally tough."

That strong mind-set has seen Las Cafeteras through to Canada 2015; Colombians will hope that they can maintain that outlook to perform at an even higher level when their tournament begins.

LOOK OUT FOR

NATALIA GAITAN
Born: April 3, 1991
Position: Defender

She may be small in stature, but this player rises to every occasion with her bravery and technical ability. Gaitan was captain for her country's team at the youth level before assuming the captaincy of the seniors, leading them in the FIFA Women's World Cup 2011 at just age 20. She played every minute of their three matches in Germany and was noted for having led her team in a rousing song in the tunnel before their opening match against Sweden. She also captained the team at the London 2012 Olympics and commands the respect of her peers.

NATALY ARIAS
Born: April 2, 1986
Position: Defender

Arias was an All-American midfielder at school, where she bagged tons of goals and almost as many plaudits. She captained the Terrapins women's soccer team at the University of Maryland and joined up with Colombia's national team in 2010. She participated in the FIFA Women's World Cup 2011 and the Pan American Games later that year, as well as the London 2012 Olympic Games. Arias featured at right-back and continues to impress in that position, where she is solid defensively and loves to get forward.

LADY ANDRADE
Born: January 10, 1992
Position: Midfielder/Forward

A lively player who loves nothing more than a chance to show off her dribbling skills and tricks on the big stage, Andrade was a hit at the FIFA U-20 Women's World Cup in 2010 and made the all-star team after impressing with her ability to take players on. She is still a youngster but has experience in senior international and high-level club soccer, having played in the FIFA Women's World Cup 2011 and London 2012 Olympics, as well as the Copa Libertadores Femenina and the UEFA Women's Champions League.

MEXICO

LAS TRICOLORES LOOK TO BUILD ON EXPERIENCE IN CANADA

Mexico has grown in stature in the world game since the first national women's league was set up in the late 1990s. This rising soccer nation will look to kick on again in this, its third FIFA Women's World Cup.

COACH

LEONARDO CUELLAR

Cueller is a former international midfielder who represented Mexico at the 1978 FIFA World Cup in Argentina. He played for several teams in the North American Soccer League during his career and was coaching the men's team at California State University, Los Angeles, when he was tasked with developing the women's game and coaching the national team in Mexico in the late 1990s. His dedication and enthusiasm has not wavered since. His son Christopher coaches the under-20s, and Leo is his assistant. Obsessive about the game, he once declared: "Football is my life!"

Previous outings in the tournament have shown Mexico's ability to progress as it has gone from failing to take a single point in 1999 to recording two from a brace of draws in 2011.

Coach Leonardo Cuellar, in charge of the national side in both the 1999 and 2011 editions, steered Las Tricolores to the world stage once more in 2015 and he is eager for Mexico to attain even better results this time.

"Our qualification has brought a sense of joy and relief," he said. "I am very proud of the team and the federation's commitment to women's soccer. We want to keep learning."

So far, Mexico have proved worthy scholars, the country transforming from one that once found it difficult to raise a

national women's team to one that now boasts teams capable of holding their own at all levels.

Las Tri reached the FIFA U-20 Women's World Cup quarterfinals in 2010 and 2012, and that feat was equaled by the under-17 in their edition of the competition in 2014.

The senior team is now packed with graduates from those U-20 tournaments, and they were utilized to good effect in their regional qualifying competition, the CONCACAF Women's Championship, in October 2014.

Although Mexico stuttered in its opener

Mexico is as dedicated to developing its game as the team's long-serving coach Leonardo Cuellar.

KEY PLAYER

ALINA GARCIAMENDEZ
Born: April 16, 1991

A Texas-raised central defender who is strong in the air, technically impressive, and a natural leader, Garciamendez was a stand-out success for Stanford University during her college career. A star for Mexico's under-20s side, she scored against Nigeria in the FIFA U-20 Women's World Cup 2010 to level the match 1–1 and see her team through to the knockout stages, for the first time, as group winners. A starter for Mexico in the FIFA Women's World Cup 2011, she has played in the German Frauen-Bundesliga with 1. FFC Frankfurt, where her teammates included FIFA Women's World Cup 2007 winners Fatmire Alushi and Melanie Behringer. She is studying at a dental school in Texas.

WORLD CUP RECORD

Year	Venue	Result
1991	China	Did not qualify
1995	Sweden	Did not qualify
1999	USA	Group stage (4th, Group B)
2003	USA	Did not qualify
2007	China	Did not qualify
2011	Germany	Group stage (3rd, Group B)

th a 1–0 loss to Costa Rica, Cuellar uffled his pack, and they went on to molish Martinique 10–0 before disposing Jamaica 3–1. The coach rested players in e semifinal against the USA, which ended a 3–0 defeat, but that decision ultimately id dividends when his team beat Trinidad d Tobago in extra time in the match for rd place.

That result assured Mexico of a qualification for Canada 2015, and Cuellar said he hoped his squad would do its confederation proud on the world stage.

Mexico still has some way to go to make the kind of impact that fellow CONCACAF representative the USA has had on the competition. Yet with many of his players competing for American colleges or in

that country's National Women's Soccer league, Las Tricolores are learning fast. And although the squad is less physically imposing than its rivals, the team counters any potential shortfall with tenacity and technique.

When they run out in Canada this summer, Cuellar's ever-improving squad just might teach the world a few lessons of its own.

LOOK OUT FOR

VERONICA PEREZ
Born: May 18, 1988
Position: Midfielder

Perez hails from California and appeared for the USA under-23s. She switched to Mexico in 2009 and ironically scored the winning goal for Las Tri in their 2–1 semifinal win over the Stars and Stripes in the CONCACAF Women's World Cup qualifying competition in 2010. She helps build attacks but also likes to get forward with dangerous runs into the penalty area. She has played college soccer for the University of Washington's Huskies and professionally in America with three different teams.

MARIBEL DOMINGUEZ
Born: November 18, 1978
Position: Forward

Dominguez pretended to be a boy so that she could play the beautiful game as a child in Mexico City. She played in the FIFA Women's World Cup 1999 in the USA and has now accrued well over 100 caps. Sometimes referred to as "Marigol" for her scoring exploits, she holds the distinction of being the only player to have scored for Mexico in the Olympic Games, FIFA Women's World Cup, CONCACAF Women's Championship, and Pan American Games. She is credited with making soccer popular in her homeland.

MONICA OCAMPO
Born: January 4, 1987
Position: Forward

Ocampo is a clever player with a sweet left foot—although it was with her right that she scored a stunning long-range equalizer against England in the FIFA Women's World Cup 2011. She is reliable in front of the goal and will take her chances when they come. She has forged a career across the border, first in the USA's W-League, before turning out for Women's Professional Soccer league team Atlanta Beat and Sky Blue FC in the National Women's Soccer League. She was top scorer for Sky Blue in 2013.

FIFA WOMEN'S WORLD CUP HISTORY

The first official FIFA Women's World Cup was held in China in 1991, with just 12 teams present. Although Canada will host only the seventh edition of the tournament, many memorable moments and stars have been created in its 24-year history. In total, 24 national teams have featured in the finals, playing in 180 matches. This section chronicles every result and group table—from the USA's triumphant "triple-edged sword" attack in 1991 to Japan's penalty shoot-out heroines in 2011.

One of the most iconic images of FIFA Women's World Cups past—a shirtless Brandi Chastain drops to her knees in celebration of her trophy-winning penalty kick in 1999.

FIFA WOMEN'S WORLD CUP CHINA 1991

Following the success of the FIFA 1988 International Women's Tournament in China, teams returned to Guangdong three years later to compete for the first official world title.

Women's soccer captured the public imagination on a global scale in 1991 when the inaugural official FIFA Women's World Championship kicked off in China. More than half a million fans turned out to watch 12 teams compete for honors across five stadiums in Guangdong Province in southeast China.

The final, between pre-tournament favorites USA and Norway at Guangzhou's Tianhe Stadium, remains one of the most nail-biting in the 24-year history of the competition. Matches were 80 minutes long for this tournament rather than soccer's standard 90, and the battle between the Stars and Stripes and its greatest rivals was so close that extra time was almost needed.

Star player and tournament Golden Shoe winner Michelle Akers got Anson Dorrance's USA team off to a flying start 20 minutes into the final with a stupendous header, but Norway's leading scorer of the tournament, Linda Medalen, equalized nine minutes lat[er]. The 63,000 spectators watched breathless[ly] as the game remained deadlocked and the clock ticked down, but with two minutes to go Akers leaped on a weak Norwegian bac[k] pass to side-foot it into an empty net and secure a historic victory for the USA.

Julie Foudy (left), Michelle Akers (center), a[nd] Player of the Tournament Carin Jennings li[ft] the trophy and a bouquet of flowers.

aly striker Carolina Morace, who would
on to manage Canada at a FIFA Women's
rld Cup and coach a men's team in Italy's
e C, made history when she hit the
mpetition's first-ever hat trick.

was a historic tournament for women
cials, too, as female referees and
stants featured for the first time in a FIFA
mpetition, with Claudia Vasconcelos of
zil taking the whistle in the third-place
yoff between Sweden and Germany.
at match finished 4–0 to the
ndinavians, whose roster included star
er Pia Sundhage, who 20 years later
uld coach the USA in the FIFA Women's
rld Cup 2011. Germany, whose squad
uded a 27-year-old Silvia Neid, went on
ft the FIFA Fair Play award.

l told, 99 goals flew in during the 26
ches of the tournament, with the USA,
turing a 19-year-old Mia Hamm and
year-old students Julie Foudy and Kristine
, top-scoring in the tournament with 25
e conceding just five.

GROUP A

China PR	4	Norway	0
Denmark	3	New Zealand	0
China PR	2	Denmark	2
Norway	4	New Zealand	0
China PR	4	New Zealand	1
Norway	2	Denmark	1

	P	W	D	L	F	A	Pts
China PR	3	2	1	0	10	3	5
Norway	3	2	0	1	6	5	4
Denmark	3	1	1	1	6	4	3
New Zealand	3	0	0	3	1	11	0

GROUP B

Japan	0	Brazil	1
Sweden	2	USA	3
Japan	0	Sweden	8
Brazil	0	USA	5
Japan	0	USA	3
Brazil	0	Sweden	2

	P	W	D	L	F	A	Pts
USA	3	3	0	0	11	2	6
Sweden	3	2	0	1	12	3	4
Brazil	3	1	0	2	1	7	2
Japan	3	0	0	3	0	12	0

GROUP C

Chinese Taipei	0	Italy	5
Germany	4	Nigeria	0
Chinese Taipei	0	Germany	3
Italy	1	Nigeria	0
Chinese Taipei	2	Nigeria	0
Italy	0	Germany	2

	P	W	D	L	F	A	Pts
Germany	3	3	0	0	9	0	6
Italy	3	2	0	1	6	2	4
Chinese Taipei	3	1	0	2	2	8	2
Nigeria	3	0	0	3	0	7	0

QUARTERFINALS

China PR	0	Sweden	1
Norway	3	Italy	2*
Denmark	1	Germany	2*
USA	7	Chinese Taipei	0

After extra time

SEMIFINALS

Sweden	1	Norway	4
Germany	2	USA	5

THIRD-PLACE MATCH

Sweden	4	Germany	0

FINAL – November 30: Tianhe Stadium, Guangzhou

Norway	1	USA	2
Medalen (29)		Akers (20)	
Akers (78)			

H-T: 1–1   **Att:** 63,000   **Ref:** Zhuk (Belarus)

Norway: Seth, Zaborowski (Straedet 79), Espeseth, Nyborg, Carlsen, Haugen, Store, Riise, Medalen, Hegstad, Svensson
USA: Harvey, Heinrichs, Higgins, Overbeck, Hamilton, Hamm, Akers, Foudy, Jennings, Lilly, Fawcett
Top scorers: 10 Akers (USA), 7 Mohr (Germany), 6 Medalen (Norway), 6 Jennings (USA)

batic action from Italy's 5–0 opening
inst Chinese Taipei in the group stage.

FIFA WOMEN'S WORLD CUP SWEDEN 1995

A longtime hotbed of women's soccer, Sweden proved enthusiastic hosts when the second global tournament came to Europe and Scandinavia provided the first European winners.

"The future is feminine," declared then FIFA general secretary Joseph S. Blatter after the second edition of the FIFA Women's World Cup had come to a close in Sweden in the summer of 1995.

His pronouncement was not without foundation: more than 110,000 supporters had just witnessed 26 keenly contested matches between 12 of the world's top women's teams. Up-and-coming stars such as China PR's Sun Wen, USA's Mia Hamm, and Germany's Maren Meinert had all

graced the world stage with their skills.

Furthermore, Swedish official Ingrid Jonsson had become the first woman to referee a FIFA final, while two of the game's future greats, then-teenagers Birgit Prinz of Germany and Japan's Homare Sawa, tasted a World Cup environment for the very first time.

Parity with the men's game had come, too, with matches now lasting 90 minutes—and supporters across Sweden savored every moment of them as 99 goals billowed into the nets in the space of two weeks.

The host did not feature for the full fortnight of competition, however. Despite bouncing back from a shock opening-mat defeat by Brazil, Sweden was eliminated I China in the quarterfinals in the first-ever FIFA Women's World Cup match to be decided by penalties.

England, whose squad featured future

Germany striker Heidi Mohr and Brazil's Cenira compete for the ball as Sissi looks in Germany's 6–1 group stage win.

nager Hope Powell, and Japan were
aten by Germany and the USA in their
arters, which left Denmark needing to
ercome Norway.

was quite an ask: the Norwegians had
wered their way through the group stage,
ting 17 goals without reply, and though
nmark scored the only goal Norway
uld concede, it lost the quarterfinal 3–1.

purred on by vociferous Scandinavian
port, Norway went on to avenge its 1991
al defeat to USA in the semis, with Golden
e winner Ann Kristin Aarones scoring the
y goal to beat the holders.

hina PR's hopes of reaching this edition's
al, meanwhile, were dashed in the 88th
nute of its semi against Germany when
tina Wiegmann popped up to score the
nner.

he rain fell steadily on the first all-
ropean FIFA Women's World Cup final,
t nothing could dampen Norway's title
, which was settled by goals from the
remely gifted midfielder Hege Riise and
0-year-old Marianne Pettersen in front of
re than 17,000 fans.

rway's "supremely gifted" midfielder
ge Riise gets her hands on the
veted prize.

GROUP A

Sweden	0	Brazil	1
Germany	1	Japan	0
Sweden	3	Germany	2
Brazil	1	Japan	2
Sweden	2	Japan	0
Brazil	1	Germany	6

	P	W	D	L	F	A	Pts
Germany	3	2	0	1	9	4	6
Sweden	3	2	0	1	5	3	6
Japan	3	1	0	2	2	4	3
Brazil	3	1	0	2	3	8	3

GROUP B

Norway	8	Nigeria	0
England	3	Canada	2
Norway	2	England	0
Nigeria	3	Canada	3
Norway	7	Canada	0
Nigeria	2	England	3

	P	W	D	L	F	A	Pts
Norway	3	3	0	0	17	0	9
England	3	2	0	1	6	6	6
Canada	3	0	1	2	5	13	1
Nigeria	3	0	1	2	5	14	1

GROUP C

USA	3	China PR	3
Denmark	5	Australia	0
USA	2	Denmark	0
China PR	4	Australia	2
USA	4	Australia	1
China PR	3	Denmark	1

	P	W	D	L	F	A	Pts
USA	3	2	1	0	9	4	7
China PR	3	2	1	0	10	6	7
Denmark	3	1	0	2	6	5	3
Australia	3	0	0	3	3	13	0

QUARTERFINALS

Germany	3	England	0
Sweden	1 (3)	China PR	1 (4)*
Japan	0	USA	4
Norway	3	Denmark	1

* After extra time (pens)

SEMIFINALS

Germany	1	China PR	0
USA	0	Norway	1

THIRD-PLACE MATCH

China PR	0	USA	2

FINAL – June 18: Rasunda Stadium, Solna

Germany	0	Norway	2

Riise (37)
Pettersen (40)

H-T: 0–2 **Att:** 17,158 **Ref:** Jonsson (Sweden)

Germany: Goller, Bernhard, Austermuhl, Pohlmann (Wunderlich 75), Lohn, Meinert (Smisek 86), Voss-Tecklenburg, Wiegmann, Mohr, Neid, Prinz (Brocker 42)
Norway: Nordby, Svensson, Espeseth, A. Nymark Andersen, N. Nymark Andersen, Riise, Haugen, Medalen, Aarones, Myklebust, Pettersen
Top scorers: 6 Aarones (Norway), 5 Riise (Norway)

FIFA WOMEN'S WORLD CUP USA 1999

With two years of planning and marketing behind the promotion of the FIFA Women's World Cup, the USA's organizers believed that the 1999 competition could be big. Boy, were they righ

As breakthrough competitions go, the third edition of the FIFA Women's World Cup has to rank among the most significant.

The USA went all out to make this tournament a success, and the public responded with the same enthusiasm: spectators filed through the turnstiles in the hundreds of thousands, host cities embraced visiting teams, and television viewers tuned in to watch the tournament in the millions. Women's soccer was on the map, and deservedly so.

Host and reigning Olympic champion the USA scored 18 goals and conceded just three on its road to a gripping final against China PR. Brazil's flair player Sissi and China's shining talent Sun Wen bagged seven goals apiece to jointly claim the Golden Shoe.

In total, a whacking 123 goals were scored across the board as the 16 teams played their hearts out under the most intense public gaze and media glare yet experienced in the women's game.

Oh, and USA midfielder Brandi Chastain whipped off her shirt after scoring the winning penalty in the final against China PR to create an iconic and enduring image 20th-century sports.

The USA did not have it all its own way on home turf, though. The Stars and Stripe had to come back from 2–1 down to beat reigning European champions Germany

This is what 90,185 fans at a FIFA Women's World Cup Final looks like.

the quarterfinals.

ny DiCicco's team was back in its stride
he semifinals, easing past Brazil, who had
yed the tournament of a lifetime after
ning just once in each of the previous
FIFA Women's World Cups.

hina saw off Russia 2–0 in the quarters,
it blitzed holders Norway 5–0 in the
i on July 4 in Foxborough en route to
final. That defeat brought an end to the
wegians' remarkable record of 10 straight
Women's World Cup victories.

nalists China and the USA eventually
h met their match when they went head
ead in the 1994 FIFA World Cup final
ue, the Rose Bowl in Pasadena, six days
r.

hina had lost 2–1 to the USA in the
-ever Women's Olympic final three years
ier on American soil. But in the 1999 final
re was little to choose between the two
0,185 spectators (a record for a women's
rting event) were kept on the edge of their
ts into extra time and penalties, with the
ch and the title settled in the USA's favor
nks to a Briana Scurry save and Chastain's
lness under pressure.

A president Sepp Blatter and president/
of the FIFA Women's World Cup 1999
anizing Committee Marla Messing are
wded out by the raised arms of the
torious US team.

GROUP A

USA	3	Denmark	0
Korea DPR	1	Nigeria	2
USA	7	Nigeria	1
Korea DPR	3	Denmark	1
USA	3	Korea DPR	0
Nigeria	2	Denmark	0

	P	W	D	L	F	A	Pts
USA	3	3	0	0	13	1	9
Nigeria	3	2	0	1	5	8	6
Korea DPR	3	1	0	2	4	6	3
Denmark	3	0	0	3	1	8	0

GROUP B

Germany	1	Italy	1
Brazil	7	Mexico	1
Germany	6	Mexico	0
Brazil	2	Italy	0
Germany	3	Brazil	3
Mexico	0	Italy	2

	P	W	D	L	F	A	Pts
Brazil	3	2	1	0	12	4	7
Germany	3	1	2	0	10	4	5
Italy	3	1	1	1	3	3	4
Mexico	3	0	0	3	1	15	0

GROUP C

Norway	2	Russia	1
Japan	1	Canada	1
Norway	7	Canada	1
Japan	0	Russia	5
Norway	4	Japan	0
Canada	1	Russia	4

	P	W	D	L	F	A	Pts
Norway	3	3	0	0	13	2	9
Russia	3	2	0	1	10	3	6
Canada	3	0	1	2	3	12	1
Japan	3	0	1	2	1	10	1

GROUP D

China PR	2	Sweden	1
Australia	1	Ghana	1
China PR	7	Ghana	0
Australia	1	Sweden	3
China PR	3	Australia	1
Ghana	0	Sweden	2

	P	W	D	L	F	A	Pts
China PR	3	3	0	0	12	2	9
Sweden	3	2	0	1	6	3	6
Australia	3	0	1	2	3	7	1
Ghana	3	0	1	2	1	10	1

QUARTERFINALS

USA	3	Germany	2
Brazil	4	Nigeria	3*
Norway	3	Sweden	1
China PR	2	Russia	0

* After extra time

SEMIFINALS

USA	2	Brazil	0
Norway	0	China PR	5

THIRD-PLACE MATCH

Brazil	0 (5)	Norway	0 (4)*

* On penalties

FINAL – July 10: Rose Bowl, Pasadena

USA	0 (5)	China PR	0 (4)	After extra time (pens)

H-T: 0–0; F-T: 0–0   Att: 90,185   Ref: Petignat (Switzerland)

USA: Scurry, Overbeck, Chastain, Hamm, Akers (Whalen 91), Foudy, Parlow (MacMillan 57), Lilly, Fawcett, Milbrett (Venturini 115), Markgraf
China PR: Gao, Wang, Fan, Zhao (Qiu 114), Jin (Xie 119), Sun, Liu A., Pu (Zhang 59), Wen, Liu Y., Bai
Top scorers: 7 Sun (China PR), 7 Sissi (Brazil), 4 Aarones (Norway)

FIFA WOMEN'S WORLD CUP USA 2003

The USA stepped in at a late stage to host the best teams from around the world for a second successive occasion, but it would not be a case of repeated success for them on the field.

The 2003 SARS virus crisis that affected chosen host China meant that in May of that year the FIFA Women's World Cup finals were reluctantly switched to the USA.

It was the second consecutive time that America had played host—and that autumn the USA rose to the challenge. Despite the tournament clashing with the wildly popular American football and baseball seasons, the crowds still came in the hundreds of thousands to watch the women in venues in the east and west of the country.

They were richly rewarded. Thirty-somethings Sun Wen of China PR, Germany's Maren Meinert, and Mia Hamm of the USA continued to thrill, but legends in the making such as Brazil's Marta, the USA's Abby Wambach, and Germany's Kerstin Garefrekes also stood out despite their relative youth.

There were new faces among the 16 teams, too, with France, Korea Republic, and Argentina making their FIFA Women's World Cup debuts.

The usual suspects—USA, Germany, Norway, Sweden, and China—all progressed to the quarterfinals. Russia, whose squad included the youngest player of the tournament in 16-year-old talent Elena Danilova, also made the last eight, along with Brazil and Canada, with the North Americans progressing beyond the

Golden goal-scorer Nia Kunzer puts her hands to her head in disbelief as she reacts to winning the 2003 final.

...ges for the first time.

...he Canucks, with 20-year-old star striker ...istine Sinclair leading the line, ended ...na's World Cup with a 1–0 quarterfinal ...ory in only their second win over the ...el Roses, who went on to collect the FIFA ...r Play award.

...ermany signaled its intent with a 7–1 ...nolition of Russia in Portland, and the USA ...off old adversaries Norway with lively ...prospect Wambach scoring the only ...l. Sweden beat Brazil 2–1, although a ...year-old Marta kept a cool head, despite ...tender years, to score from the spot.

...the semifinals in Portland, Germany ...ninated USA 3–0, inflicting only the ...ond-ever FIFA Women's World Cup defeat ...the hosts. Canada's dreams of a final on ...soil were ended by Sweden, who came ...ck from behind with two late goals.

...he winning goal for Germany in the final ...ainst Sweden in Los Angeles was of the ...den variety, with Nia Kunzer scoring a ...werful header in the 98th minute to cap ...a German comeback.

...t was only the second golden goal ever ...be scored at a FIFA Women's World Cup, ...d it would be the last, but what a crucial ...al it was.

...tablished stars such as Mia Hamm ...mbined with emerging talents like her ...A striker partner Abby Wambach.

GROUP A

Nigeria	0	Korea DPR	3
USA	3	Sweden	1
Sweden	1	Korea DPR	0
USA	5	Nigeria	0
Sweden	3	Nigeria	0
Korea DPR	0	USA	3

	P	W	D	L	F	A	Pts
USA	3	3	0	0	11	1	9
Sweden	3	2	0	1	5	3	6
Korea DPR	3	1	0	2	3	4	3
Nigeria	3	0	0	3	0	11	0

GROUP B

Norway	2	France	0
Brazil	3	Korea Republic	0
Norway	1	Brazil	4
France	1	Korea Republic	0
Korea Republic	1	Norway	7
France	1	Brazil	1

	P	W	D	L	F	A	Pts
Brazil	3	2	1	0	8	2	7
Norway	3	2	0	1	10	5	6
France	3	1	1	1	2	3	4
Korea Republic	3	0	0	3	1	11	0

GROUP C

Germany	4	Canada	1
Japan	6	Argentina	0
Germany	3	Japan	0
Canada	3	Argentina	0
Canada	3	Japan	1
Argentina	1	Germany	6

	P	W	D	L	F	A	Pts
Germany	3	3	0	0	13	2	9
Canada	3	2	0	1	7	5	6
Japan	3	1	0	2	7	6	3
Argentina	3	0	0	3	1	15	0

GROUP D

Australia	1	Russia	2
China PR	1	Ghana	0
Ghana	0	Russia	3
China PR	1	Australia	1
Ghana	2	Australia	1
China PR	1	Russia	0

	P	W	D	L	F	A	Pts
China PR	3	2	1	0	3	1	7
Russia	3	2	0	1	5	2	6
Ghana	3	1	0	2	2	5	3
Australia	3	0	1	2	3	5	1

QUARTERFINALS

USA	1	Norway	0
Brazil	1	Sweden	2
Germany	7	Russia	1
China PR	0	Canada	1

SEMIFINALS

USA	0	Germany	3
Sweden	2	Canada	1

THIRD-PLACE MATCH

USA	3	Canada	1

FINAL – October 12: Home Depot Center, Carson

Germany	2	Sweden	1	After extra time
Meinert (46)		Ljungberg (41)		
Kunzer (98)				

H-T: 0–1; F-T: 1–1   Att: 26,137   Ref: Babadac (Romania)

Germany: Rottenberg, Stegemann, Lingor, Wunderlich (Kunzer 88), Prinz, Wiegmann, Minnert, Meinert, Hingst, Garefrekes (Muller 76), Gottschlich
Sweden: Jonsson, Westberg, Tornqvist, Marklund, Mostrom, Larsson (Bengtsson 76), Andersson (Sjogran 53), Ljungberg, Svensson, Sjostrom (Fagerstrom 53), Ostberg
Top scorers: 7 Prinz (Germany), 4 Meinert (Germany), 4 Katia (Brazil), 4 Garefrekes (Germany)

FIFA WOMEN'S WORLD CUP CHINA 2007

The fifth edition was played in Asia, and around a million spectators witnessed the ever-improving standard and excitement of the women's game.

China PR finally got to stage the FIFA Women's World Cup again in the autumn of 2007, and the opening ceremony showed just how eagerly anticipated its arrival was.

Around a million spectators made their way through the turnstiles in venues across the country over the space of three weeks, and nearly 30,000 of them were lucky enough to get a ticket for the opening ceremony at Hongkou Stadium in Shanghai on September 10. Before them danced

children inside giant soccer balls and cartoonish athletic shoes, while above their heads leaped thunderous fireworks and multicolored flashing lights.

The match that followed was a spectacle, too; title holders Germany kept up the luster by obliterating Argentina 11–0 with hat tricks from Birgit Prinz, in her fourth FIFA Women's World Cup, and Sandra Smisek.

Germany faced tougher competition in its second group match when it came up

against England, which was making its firs[t] appearance at a FIFA Women's World Cup finals in 12 years.

Three days previously, England's talisma[n] striker Kelly Smith had tugged off her clea[t] and kissed them after scoring two beautif[ul] goals in a 2–2 draw with Japan. But the

A snapshot of the hugely entertaining, quirky, yet lavish opening ceremony in Shanghai.

...counter with Germany remained goalless
...spite both teams' best efforts.
...Germany enjoyed more success against
...an, winning 2–0 before breezing into the
...al with quarter- and semifinal wins over
...rea DPR and Norway respectively.
...Norway had been the architects of
...ina's downfall as the Steel Roses fell
...the quarterfinal stage, while Australia
...ve Brazil a scare in its quarterfinal until
...stiane bagged the winner in the 75th
...nute.
...he USA had made light work of its group,
...d it did the same with England in the
...arters, but it was beaten soundly by Brazil
...the semis in a thrilling game of skills and
...lls that saw the Chinese fans roar on
...aymaker Marta in the thousands.
...Golden Shoe and Golden Ball award
...nner Marta was unable to penetrate the
...werhouse that was Germany in the final
...Shanghai, even having a penalty saved by
...dine Angerer.
...Prinz and Simone Laudehr bagged
...cond-half goals to ensure that Germany,
...der Silvia Neid, became the first team to
...ccessfully defend the FIFA Women's World
...p title—without even conceding a goal.

**rman keeper Nadine Angerer keeps her
...narkable shutout record intact with a
...nalty save from Brazil's Marta in the final.**

GROUP A

Germany	11	Argentina	0
Japan	2	England	2
Argentina	0	Japan	1
England	0	Germany	0
Germany	2	Japan	0
England	6	Argentina	1

	P	W	D	L	F	A	Pts
Germany	3	2	1	0	13	0	7
England	3	1	2	0	8	3	5
Japan	3	1	1	1	3	4	4
Argentina	3	0	0	3	1	18	0

GROUP B

USA	2	Korea DPR	2
Nigeria	1	Sweden	1
Sweden	0	USA	2
Korea DPR	2	Nigeria	0
Nigeria	0	USA	1
Korea DPR	1	Sweden	2

	P	W	D	L	F	A	Pts
USA	3	2	1	0	5	2	7
Korea DPR	3	1	1	1	5	4	4
Sweden	3	1	1	1	3	4	4
Nigeria	3	0	1	2	1	4	1

GROUP C

Ghana	1	Australia	4
Norway	2	Canada	1
Canada	4	Ghana	0
Australia	1	Norway	1
Norway	7	Ghana	2
Australia	2	Canada	1

	P	W	D	L	F	A	Pts
Norway	3	2	1	0	10	4	7
Australia	3	1	2	0	7	4	5
Canada	3	1	1	1	7	4	4
Ghana	3	0	0	3	3	15	0

GROUP D

New Zealand	0	Brazil	5
China PR	3	Denmark	2
Denmark	2	New Zealand	0
Brazil	4	China PR	0
China PR	2	New Zealand	0
Brazil	1	Denmark	0

	P	W	D	L	F	A	Pts
Brazil	3	3	0	0	10	0	9
China PR	3	2	0	1	5	6	6
Denmark	3	1	0	2	4	4	3
New Zealand	3	0	0	3	0	9	0

QUARTERFINALS

Germany	3	Korea DPR	0
USA	3	England	0
Norway	1	China PR	0
Brazil	3	Australia	2

SEMIFINALS

Germany	3	Norway	0
USA	0	Brazil	4

THIRD-PLACE MATCH

Norway	1	USA	4

FINAL – September 30: Hongkou Football Stadium, Shanghai

Germany	2	Brazil	0

Prinz (52)
Laudehr (86)

H-T: 0–0   Att: 31,000   Ref: Ogston (Australia)

Germany: Angerer, Stegemann, Krahn, Bresonik, Behringer (Muller 74), Smisek (Alushi 80), Prinz, Lingor, Laudehr, Hingst, Garefrekes
Brazil: Andreia, Elaine, Aline (Katia 88), Tania (Pretinha 81), Renata Costa, Daniela, Formiga, Maycon, Marta, Cristiane, Ester (Rosana 63)
Top scorers: 7 Marta (Brazil), 6 Wambach (USA), 6 R. Gulbrandsen (Norway)

FIFA WOMEN'S WORLD CUP GERMANY 2011

With stands packed with noisy and colorful supporters, quality soccer throughout, and a truly astonishing finale, Germany 2011 was an outstanding experience.

Title holders and firm favorites, Germany invited the world to enjoy another "summer fairy tale"—promising to reprise the celebration of soccer that was the 2006 FIFA World Cup.

However, its dream of victory on home soil was not to be. Instead, another storybook ending was written, and a new team joined the list of giants in the game, becoming only the fourth nation to be crowned world champions.

Inspired largely by the performances and goals of its captain Homare Sawa, Japan clinched victory on penalties after a sensational final in Frankfurt against the USA.

The Nadeshiko was a popular and fitting winner not simply because of its artful passing and pressing game—it had also given its country hope following the devastating earthquake and tsunami that had affected Japan that March.

The ticket sales, investment, commercial backing, and TV and media coverage for the tournament were unprecedented. German crowds and traveling supporters packed stadiums throughout—73,680 attended the opening match pitting Germany against Canada at Berlin's Olympiastadion, creating an incredible atmosphere.

But for some late-late goals and spot-kick dramas, the lineup in the final could actually have been very different.

Japan, which had lost 2–0 to England in group play, thwarted the German juggernaut in the quarterfinals with a solitary extra-time strike by Karina Maruyama. France owed its progress to the semifinals to Elise Bussaglia

Hosts Germany played out its opening game against Canada, a 2–1 win, at Berlin Olympiastadion in front of a partisan and jubilant crowd of more than 70,000.

h-minute equalizer and some wayward
land penalties in the shoot-out that
owed.

Most astounding of all was USA versus
zil, Abby Wambach's header, in time
led on after extra time, leveling the score
2–2. The Americans buried all five of their
sequent penalty kicks, while Daiane missed
s. Marta's As Canarinhas headed home
rtbroken.

fter so much drama, the semifinals were
re straightforward, both games ending
. Sweden's attacking flow against Japan
s somewhat stunted without the injured
roline Seger, while the USA overpowered
flair of the French.

he final itself, however, was an epic. USA's
out attacking pressure was matched by
an's resistance, twice coming from behind,
e in normal time and again through Sawa
h three minutes remaining. Heart-stopping
ments included Asuza Iwashimizu's red
d after 120 minutes, Ayumi Kaihori's shoot-
saves, and Saki Kumagai's winning kick.
was a breathless and inspirational climax
a thrilling three weeks. Germany 2011
d taken the women's game to a whole
v level.

**an's talismanic captain Homare Sawa
sts the trophy to the skies after the
m's courageous triumph against the USA
an epic encounter. A country had found a
v set of heroines.**

GROUP A

Germany	2	Canada	1
Nigeria	0	France	1
Germany	1	Nigeria	0
Canada	0	France	4
France	2	Germany	4
Canada	0	Nigeria	1

	P	W	D	L	F	A	Pts
Germany	3	3	0	0	7	3	9
France	3	2	0	1	7	4	6
Nigeria	3	1	0	2	1	2	3
Canada	3	0	0	3	1	7	0

GROUP B

Japan	2	New Zealand	1
Mexico	1	England	1
Japan	4	Mexico	0
New Zealand	1	England	2
England	2	Japan	0
New Zealand	2	Mexico	2

	P	W	D	L	F	A	Pts
England	3	2	1	0	5	2	7
Japan	3	2	0	1	6	3	6
Mexico	3	0	2	1	3	7	2
New Zealand	3	0	1	2	4	6	1

GROUP C

USA	2	Korea DPR	0
Colombia	0	Sweden	1
USA	3	Colombia	0
Korea DPR	0	Sweden	1
Sweden	2	USA	1
Korea DPR	0	Colombia	0

	P	W	D	L	F	A	Pts
Sweden	3	3	0	0	4	1	9
USA	3	2	0	1	6	2	6
Korea DPR	3	0	1	2	0	3	1
Colombia	3	0	1	2	0	4	1

GROUP D

Brazil	1	Australia	0
Norway	1	Eq. Guinea	0
Brazil	3	Norway	0
Australia	3	Eq. Guinea	2
Eq. Guinea	0	Brazil	3
Australia	2	Norway	1

	P	W	D	L	F	A	Pts
Brazil	3	3	0	0	7	0	9
Australia	3	2	0	1	5	4	6
Norway	3	1	0	2	2	5	3
Eq. Guinea	3	0	0	3	2	7	0

QUARTERFINALS

Germany	0	Japan	1*
England	1 (3)	France	1 (4)*
Sweden	3	Australia	1
Brazil	2 (3)	USA	2 (5)*

*After extra time (pens)

SEMIFINALS

| Japan | 3 | Sweden | 1 |
| France | 1 | USA | 3 |

THIRD-PLACE MATCH

| Sweden | 2 | France | 1 |

FINAL – July 17: FIFA Women's World Cup Stadium, Frankfurt

| Japan | 2 (3) | USA | 2 (1)* |

Miyama (81)   Morgan (69)
Sawa (117)   Wambach (104)
H-T: 0–0; F-T: 1–1   **Att:** 48,817   **Ref:** Steinhaus (Germany)

Japan: Kaihori, Kinga, Iwashimizu, Kumagai, Sakaguchi, Ando (Ogimi 66), Miyama, Kawasumi, Sawa, Ohno (Maruyama 66; Iwabuchi 119), Sameshima. **Sent off:** Iwashimizu (120+1)
USA: Solo, Rampone, Le Peilbet, Boxx, O'Reilly, Lloyd, Krieger, Cheney (Morgan 46), Rapinoe (Heath 114), Buehler, Wambach
Top scorers: 5 Sawa (Japan), 4 Marta (Brazil), 4 Wambach (USA)

*After extra time (pens)

FIFA WOMEN'S WORLD CUP QUIZ

Test your women's soccer knowledge. There are six different sections, with five teaser in each. How many can you get right? Answers can be found at the bottom of the page. Let's kick off…

FIRSTS

1. Which tournament top scorer helped her team win the first-ever FIFA Women's World Cup by netting twice in the final against Norway?

2. Who did China beat in the 1995 quarterfinals in the first-ever FIFA Women's World Cup match to go to penalties?

3. Who was the first female coach to win the FIFA Women's World Cup?

4. Who was the first (and so far only) player to be sent off in the final of a FIFA Women's World Cup?

5. Which team earned its first-ever FIFA Women's World Cup point in 2011 when Hannah Wilkinson scored in added time against Mexico?

SECONDS

1. Which German was the second person to take a penalty in a FIFA Women's World Cup, and the first to score, in her team's 3–0 victory over Chinese Taipei?

2. Which Australian player set a FIFA Women's World Cup record for the quickest red card in the second minute of her country's final group game of 1999?

3. Who scored the second and final golden goal in FIFA Women's World Cup history to win the 2003 final?

4. Which former Sweden coach oversaw a second nation when she guided the hosts in 2007?

5. Who won the Golden Ball and Golden Shoe in 2007, as well as FIFA Women's World Player of the Year, despite only coming second in the FIFA Women's World Cup final?

GOAL-GETTERS

1. Which winning coach scored the 100th FIFA Women's World Cup goal, as a player, in 1995?

a) Silvia Neid
b) Norio Sasaki
c) Anson Dorrance

2. Which marvelous African superstar masterminded her team's first-ever victory in the FIFA Women's World Cup with a goal and an assist versus Korea DPR in 1999?

a) Perpetua Nkwocha
b) Mercy Akide
c) Genoveva Anonma

3. With 14 goals apiece, Marta and which other player are the highest-ever FIFA Women's World Cup goalscorers?

a) Birgit Prinz
b) Mia Hamm
c) Victoria Svensson

4. Who scored the latest goal in a game in FIFA Women's World Cup history to keep her team in its 2011 quarterfinal?

a) Louisa Necib
b) Abby Wambach
c) Christine Sinclair

5. Who became the oldest player to score in a FIFA Women's World Cup final, at the age of 32 years and 314 days?

a) Heidi Store
b) Katia
c) Homare Sawa

94

TOUCH LINE

Can you unscramble the five head coaches and name their team, with just the year/years they were at the FIFA Women's World Cup as a hint?

1. Main Monster (2007, 2011)
2. Reclaim A Racoon (2011)
3. Corn And Reason (1991)
4. Pushed Again (2011)
5. Hollow Peep (2007, 2011)

CHAMPIONS!

1. Who went on to win the FIFA Women's World Cup twice after first appearing in a final on the losing side as a 17-year-old?

2. Which is the only team to have featured in the semifinals of every FIFA Women's World Cup?

3. Which is the only nation to have won the FIFA Women's World Cup, the Women's Olympic Football Tournament, and the UEFA European Women's Championship?

4. Who won the Golden Ball and the Golden Boot after leading her team to FIFA Women's World Cup glory in her fifth finals appearance?

5. Which two nations will be vying to win the FIFA Women's World Cup for a record third time in 2015?

MEMORABLE MOMENTS

1. Who is this unusual figure in goal against Denmark in 1995?

2. Who saved a penalty to help her team win the FIFA Women's World Cup in 1999?

3. When her country scored in its first FIFA Women's World Cup in 12 years, who celebrated in style?

4. Who spearheaded the shock of the 2007 tournament as the United States lost in the semifinals?

5. Whose nose was broken in the opening match of the FIFA Women's World Cup 2011?

KEY NOTES FOR THE MATCH SCHEDULE (PP. 16–17)

Notes for deciding the group stages
P = played (each team plays three group matches); W = won; D = draw; L = lost; F = goals scored (for); A = goals conceded (against); Pts = points. Three points for a win; one for a draw; no points for a loss.

After most points, groups are decided first by better positive goal difference, then the total goals scored. After this, the head-to-head results will decide the order. If three teams are involved, again the goal difference in these matches decides, then the total goals scored. If teams are still equal, then the FIFA Organising Committee will use a lottery to draw teams.

Explanation of knockout stages
All knockout matches will be decided on the day they are played. If the scores are even after 90 minutes, extra time (two 15-minute periods) will be allotted for play. If the scores again remain even, penalty kicks (a penalty shoot-out) will decide the winner. Teams will take five shots each, alternately, unless one team cannot win after three or four attempts. If the scores are still even after 10 attempts, then a sudden-death shoot-out follows, decided by the first team to score.

The alphanumeric designations in the second round—the Round of 16—refer to first-round group positions. 1A is the winner of Group A, 2F is the runner-up in Group F. The four third-placed teams with the best records in the first round will join the group winners and the runners-up. The third-placed teams will play the winner of a group other than the one in which they have already played.

The match numbers for the subsequent rounds (shown in parentheses above each game slot) are the official tournament match numbers. W before the number refers to the winners of that tie (L denotes losers), thus the first semifinal, match 49, will be between the winners of quarterfinal matches 45 and 46.

AUTHORS' ACKNOWLEDGEMENTS
Compiling this book would not have been possible without the assistance of the following generous people and supporters of the women's game, so we offer our gratitude to: Kevin Ashby, Jennifer Ast, Cintia Barlem, David Barber, Sven Beyrich, Peter Davis, Nicola Demaine, Tony DiCicco, Moya Dodd, Carolina Garcia, Scott Gleba, Paul Green, Aaron Heifetz, Markus Helbling, Fran Hilton-Smith, Jeremy Ruane, Paul Saffer, Ruth Scheithauer, Dawn Scott, Richard Scott, Alex Stone, Julie Teo, Steven Upfold, the-afc.com, canadasoccer.com, concacaf.com, conmebol.com, fifa.com, and uefa.com

CREDITS

The publishers would like to thank the following sources for their kind permission to reproduce the pictures this book.

Action Images: p. 77 (Henry Romero/Reuters). Andes: p. 48 (Right: Carlos Rodriguez). Canada Soccer: p. 8 (Andre Ringuette). Corbis: p. 10 (Sigi Tischler/EPA). Federación Costarricense de Fútbol: p. 68 (Left). Fédéra Ivoirienne de Football: p. 34 (Right). Getty Images: p. 4 (Mike Hewitt), 6–7 (Ellen Atkin/Design Pics), 9 (Kevin C. Cox), 11 (Mitchell Leff), 12 (Kevin C. Cox), 14 (Cole Burston/AFP), 15 (Alexander Hassenstein), 18–19 (Thorste Wagner), 20–21 (Kevin C. Cox), 22 (Right: Paul Ellis/AFP), 22 (Left: Graham Stuart/AFP), 23 (David Cooper/Toron Star), 24 (Right: Matt King), 24 (Left: Stanley Chou), 25 (Stanley Chou), 26 (Right: Atsushi Tomura), 26 (Left: Star Chou), 28–29 (VI Images), 32 (Right: Jeff Vinnick), 32 (Left: Andreas Froeberg/Bongarts), 33 (Thomas Neidermue Bongarts), 34 (Left: Alexander Hassenstein), 36 (Jose Joao Sa/Bongarts), 37 (Martin Rose), 38–39 (Staney Chou) 40–41 (Derek Leung), 42 (Hong Wu), 43 (Stanley Chou), 44 (Right: Lance King), 44 (Left: Alexander Hassenstein Bongarts), 45 (Grant Halverson), 46 (Right: Joern Pollex), 46 (Left: Julian Finney), 48 (Left: Alexander Hassenstein 49 (Juan Cevallos/AFP), 50–51 (Tom Szczerbowski), 52 (Right: Mitchell Leff), 52 (Left: Brian Blanco), 53 (Cooper Neill), 54 (Right: Chris Hyde), 54 (Left: Stanley Chou), 55 (Bradley Kanaris), 56 (Jonathan Nackstrand/AFP), 57 (Jonathan Nackstrand/AFP), 58 (Right: Friedemann Vogel/Bongarts), 58 (Left: Martin Rose), 59 (Richard Wolowi 60–61(Martin Rose), 62 (Right: John Berry), 62 (Left: Evaristo Sa/AFP), 63 (Yasuyoshi Chiba/AFP), 64 (Right: Suhaimi Abdullah), 64 (Left: Alexander Hassenstein); 65 (Stanley Chou), 66–67 (Claudio Villa), 68 (Right: Michae Thomas), 69 (Mitchell Leff), 70–71 (Alex Grimm), 72 (Right: Sebastien Bozon/AFP), 72 (Left: Francois Nascimber AFP), 73 (Francois Lo Presti/AFP), 74 (Right: Kieran Galvin/Anadolu Agency), 74 (Left: Stu Forster), 75 (Nigel Roddis), 76 (Right: Robert Cianflone), 76 (Left: Martin Rose), 78 (Right: Patrick McDermott), 78 (Left: George Fre 79 (Boris Streubel/Bongarts), 80–81 (Robert Beck/Sports Illustrated), 82–83 (Tommy Cheng/AFP), 85 (Alexander Hassenstein), 84 (Bongarts), 86 (Robert Beck/Sports Illustrated), 87 (Crala Overbeck/AFP), 88 (Hector Mata/AFP) 89 (Al Messerschmidt), 90 (Mark Ralston/AFP), 91 (Christof Koepsel/Bongarts), 92 (Odd Andersen/AFP), 93 (Pat Stollarz/AFP), 95 (Top left: George Tiedemann/Sports Illustrated), 95 (Top right: Timothy A. Clary/AFP), 95 (Bottom left: Paul Gilham), 95 (Bottom center: Mark Ralston/AFP), 95 (Bottom right: Alex Livesey), 96 (Mike Hewitt). The Namibian: 35 (Helge Schutz). Press Association Images: 27 (Jay LaPrete/AP), 30–31 (Willie Vass/Ranger FC), 47 (Empics Sport).

Every effort has been made to acknowledge correctly and contact the source and/or copyright holder of eac picture, and Abbeville Press apologizes for any unintentional errors or omissions, which will be corrected in future editions of this book.

A young Canadian fan cheers on her team at the FIFA U-20 Women's World Cup Canada 201 Now her nation will welcome the best in the world in the senior women's game.